D0235680

First published 2018 by
EZ PUBLISHING
www.ezpublishing.ie

Texts © Ciarán Deeney and David Clarke
Foreword © John Creedon
Photographs © National Treasures

ISBN 978 1 5272 2844 3

A CIP record is available from the British Library.

1 3 5 7 9 10 8 6 4 2

Logo Design: Donn Maguire
Photography: Pearl Phelan, Eoin O'Conaill, Andres Poveda,
Eoin Cooke, Ciarán Deeney, David Clarke

Set in Slate Pro
Book production by Hi Tone Books
Design by Niall McCormack
Printed in Poland by L&C Printing

# NATIONAL TREASURES

## A PEOPLES' ARCHIVE

Compiled by **CIARÁN DEENEY** and **DAVID CLARKE**

Foreword by JOHN CREEDON

EZ

# NATIONAL TREASURES

## A PEOPLES' ARCHIVE

**National Treasures** explores the history of Ireland over the past 100 years using cherished objects in the hands of members of the public. Collected from the four corners of Ireland, this book is a selection of historical objects submitted by people from all walks of life and it reveals the many diverse histories upon our island.

**Ciarán Deeney** and **David Clarke** have worked together for over ten years producing documentary, drama and multi-platform projects including National Treasures.

**www.nationaltreasures.ie**

## NATIONAL TREASURES PARTNERS

museum
National Museum of Ireland
Ard-Mhúsaem na hÉireann

# Foreword

From the very beginning of National Treasures, all of us all wondered if we could successfully deliver such a big project across so many platforms in such a short period of time. More importantly, we wondered if people would grasp the concept and contribute their private belongings, many of which would be highly charged with emotions and family histories. Well, not only did the people of Ireland grasp it, they embraced it.

*National Treasures* brought me back to a two-year Diploma Course I took at an Roinn Béaloideas some years ago in UCC. Béaloideas can be translated as 'mouth teaching', which is the oral tradition of learning through conversation. In that regard, we can safely say that National Treasures has sparked thousands of conversations.

Firstly, there was the day-long hub-bub of a hundred simultaneous conversations at our roadshows, where people queued up, sometimes for hours, to tell their stories and present the evidence. In many cases, stories previously untold (like the secret grenade factory beneath the Ford Motor Plant in Cork) got a first public outing. The project has prompted conversations in front rooms, pubs, taxis, classrooms and, of course, on social media.

A daughter of mine, with a third level education and two little girls of her own was moved to ask me, "Who was Frank Ryan and why were the Irish fighting in the Spanish Civil War?" In my explanation, I recalled that 'Red' Mick O'Riordan, the Irish communist leader, was a cousin of ours and a great pal of her grandfather's.

Now, that conversation and the story of that family connection would have been wasted on her when she was younger and, had she not seen the Frank Ryan item, then the story would have gone untold. It would have disappeared and slipped between the cracks of generations in a family.

There is real credit due to Ciarán Deeney and Dave Clarke for imagining such an all-embracing project. Similarly, the Broadcasting Authority of Ireland, the National Museum of Ireland, and RTÉ must be credited, not only for seeing the possibilities of such an idea, but for wholeheartedly nurturing and supporting it from beginning to end.

In his song, 'Heaven Knows', Jimmy McCarthy speaks of 'the glory of a song set free, a song sung over and over'. In other words, a song sheet sitting in a closed drawer is inert, lifeless. However, when someone draws breath and breathes life into it, the song lives.

The same is true of our stories. They must also be set free and they must be told over and over. In that regard, the people of Ireland have brought life to many narratives, each one adding another thread to the weave that forms the tapestry of Ireland and the Irish. *National Treasures* was a 'meitheal násiúnta', a national co-operative, driven by the creators, curators, crew, and contributors. Like any meitheal, everyone who contributed can now feel satisfaction with a job well done.

JOHN CREEDON

# Introduction

National Treasures is a social history project authored by members of the public across the island of Ireland. The project asked the public to dig out their own national treasures so as to have them photographed, recorded and archived, in advance of an exhibition in the National Museum of Ireland. It was launched in September 2017 and whether by submitting via our website (www.nationaltreasures.ie) or coming along to roadshows held in Galway, Cork, Dublin and Belfast, over 6,500 fascinating objects have been revealed.

Deliberately broad and open to interpretation, the project posed two questions; how do you define the "national" and what objects should be deemed "treasures"? Our goal was to create an inclusive history campaign that would be accessible for all, positive as an experience and purposely overlooked the monetary value of submitted objects. Looking at the results of this campaign, what has been created through all of these submissions is a very unusual historical archive; an archive that explores big and small histories, how the personal and national intertwine and also examines how interconnected our lives are via history and objects. This book showcases almost 200 of the objects received and the selection emphasises diversity and thematic variety.

National Treasures started out as a very simple idea. What if we were to explore the history of Ireland through objects solely in the hands of members of the public? What if we were to ignore monetary value and explore treasured objects based on their emotional and historical value alone? And what if we were to create an exhibition showcasing these items, one that emphasised the voices of the owners?

Using these questions as a starting point, we contacted RTÉ and the National Museum of Ireland who immediately rowed in behind the idea. With support from the Broadcasting Authority of Ireland following, it soon became a reality and a campaign was launched starting with a website, then turning into roadshows, a TV series, an exhibition and now ultimately a book.

A project like this wouldn't work in every country. In Ireland we are blessed with an active citizenship, people who love their history, people who take a real interest in the nuances of the story of this island and people who are willing to participate en masse in a project like this. We are very grateful to everyone who submitted to the project. In many ways, we are just the facilitators for their great stories to be told.

From our point of view, what is really exciting is that this project isn't over and it will continue to accept submissions via the website (www.nationaltreasures.ie). Upon reading this book, hopefully you will be encouraged to submit your own national treasure. We can't wait to be surprised at what still remains to be discovered. Enjoy the book, it is now your object, your story and your history.

CIARÁN DEENEY and DAVID CLARKE

# NATIONAL TREASURES

## A PEOPLES' ARCHIVE

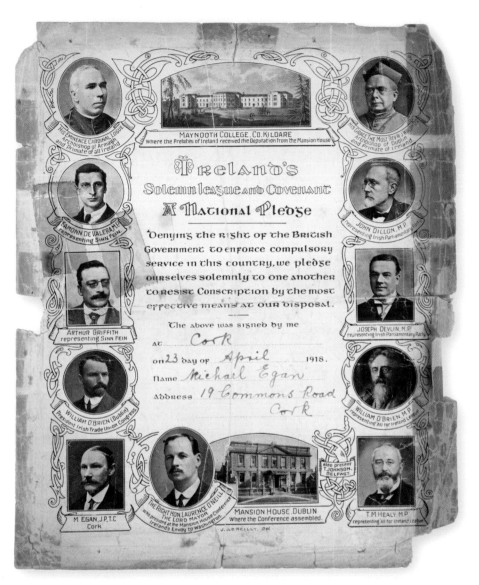

## Anti-Conscription Campaign Pledge

"This is an original copy of the anti-conscription campaign national pledge from April, 1918. Lloyd George extended conscription in England to Ireland in that year and it did not go down well. My grandfather, Michael Egan, was a member of the Irish Trade Union Congress and he represented that organisation in the campaign. This pledge was distributed throughout Ireland and people signed it in their hundreds of thousands, with some historians suggesting that it was as many as two million. The campaign, which united all shades of nationalism in Ireland, was extraordinarily successful. It was only in recent years, looking into my family history, that I fully realised the significance of this document. Not only is it a rare signed pledge, but my grandfather was also one of the nine men on the committee who created the document. He is pictured bottom left."

ALAN EGAN

**QUEEN'S COUNTY.**

Polling District of _Ballybrittas_

Sir
Madam,

Take notice that your claim to be registered as a Parliamentary and —or—Local Government Elector for above Polling District has been allowed by me.

Dated this 27th day of July, 1918.

Registration Officer,
Crown and Peace Office,
Maryborough.

To _Bridget_ _____
_Courtwood. Ballybrittas_

## 1918 Voting Registration Slip

"This is one of my most treasured possessions, a voting slip from the first time women were allowed to vote in Ireland. It is a reminder of the importance of voting and that one person, one vote did not come about easily. In this election, not every adult female was eligible to vote. Bridget must have been over 30 and had certain property rights because suffrage rights for men and women were not fully equalised until 1928. I found this voting slip in an old trunk in a house my wife and I bought. I didn't realise the significance of it when I found it, but it is only now, 100 years later, that I realise its importance. I covered up the surname because even though it's a very long time ago, I feel Bridget deserves privacy."

FRANK SMITH

## Gaudeamus Igitur
## Skull Tankard

"This celebratory skull tankard is from Germany. It is made of porcelain and has a Latin inscription on it that reads 'Gaudeamus Igitur', which means let us be joyful. The tankard is used in traditional graduation ceremonies along with a drinking song encouraging drinkers from this tankard to be joyful while they are still young. The image of the skull is to remind drinkers of what we are all to become very shortly. It is a family heirloom and has been used by generations of people who have enjoyed life."

MARY BOISSEL

PLATE 23.

## Atlas and Cyclopedia of Ireland

"This book has been in the family for a long time and is an original edition, not a reprint, of approximately 250 pages. On the cover there is a woman playing the harp, with an Irish wolfhound looking on from behind. The book is divided into two parts: A Comprehensive Delineation of the Thirty-Two Counties, by P.W. Joyce, and the General History as told by A.M. Sullivan and continued by P. D. Nunan. There are many pictures throughout the book, including one of a Celtic cross, and Irish family names and coats of arms. I think the colour images are in quite an extraordinary condition for a book of its age. It's a family heirloom and very important to me."

JOHN SHANNY

## Galway Shawls

"This is just one item from my Galway Shawl collection. I have three brown ones and a red petticoat. I bought this one in the 1960s from Mrs Elwoods' Pawn Shop on Quay Street in Galway when I was a young woman. The shawl was probably made around the turn of the century and I believe many of these were actually produced in Paisley in Scotland. I have always had a love and fascination of the past and I have memories of donkeys and carts passing by our window on the way to market and the women selling eggs and wearing beautiful shawls like these. For me, they illustrate a unique aspect of our heritage specific to the west of Ireland and represent the Galway I love. When I hold these shawls, I think of the strong, confident Claddagh women who wore them as they sold fish and produce at the markets in order to look after their families."

PHYLLIS MACNAMARA

## Sword from the Battle of Kinsale

"Family lore says this sword is from the Battle of Kinsale. When Hugh O'Neill's forces were retreating from the battle, they came through Sarsfield Court, Glanmire. One of O'Neill's men was injured, a young bodyguard, and left to die in Sarsfield Court. He was nursed back to health though and I am the ninth generation of his ancestors in Sarsfield Court. This sword has been in the family for generations. My great-grandfather found the sword in a ditch and connected it with the Battle of Kinsale in which our ancestors fought. The handle used to be wooden, but my mother put on the leather handle."

MAGGIE EGAN O'NEILL

## Photograph of George Walsh

"This photo I'm holding was taken in 1907 at a ball in the Mansion House for children of the city of Dublin. The child pictured is my Uncle George Walsh. He was born in 1900 in Ballsbridge Terrace, and reared in Spencer Street, North Strand. When he was only 15, George went against his family's wishes and joined the Great War, going to Liverpool we think to sign up. His father followed him over and brought him home on the grounds that he was only 15 and too young to enlist. About a year after this, however, he went again and joined the army, this time changing his name to John Kennedy and lying about his age so that he wouldn't be refused. He survived the war and lived out the remainder of his life in the UK until 1980 under the name John Kennedy. He lived a modest life working as a gardener and when I was about nine or ten, my mother took me over to Brighton where he lived to meet him. I really liked him as a person and I really like this photograph, so now it hangs on the wall in my house where it serves as a wonderful link to my family's history."

JOAN DOYLE

# Commemorative book, Guinness Staff WWI

"This beautiful bound, boxed book contains the names of Guinness employees who served during World War I, including my grandmother's brother-in-law, James (Jimmy) Cosgrove. He was originally from Portadown but resident in Dublin and employed as a cooper in Guinness. Whilst serving in the forces, he worked as a cook and did not see any action, perhaps because he had a young family back home. Although my great-aunt and he had seven children, they had no grandchildren, so my sister and I became their virtual grandchildren. This is why I have this treasured book."

ROSALEEN COLE

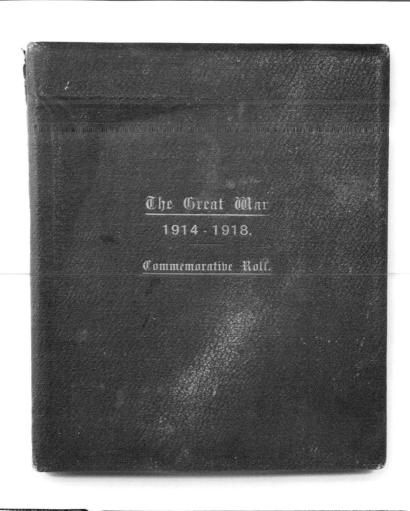

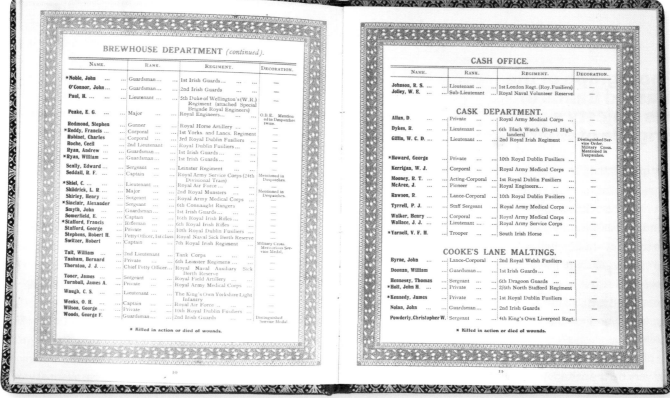

### BREWHOUSE DEPARTMENT (continued).

| NAME. | RANK. | REGIMENT. | DECORATION. |
|---|---|---|---|
| *Noble, John | Guardsman | 1st Irish Guards | — |
| O'Connor, John | Guardsman | 2nd Irish Guards | — |
| Paul, H. | Lieutenant | 5th Duke of Wellington's (W.R.) Regiment (attached Special Brigade Royal Engineers) | — |
| Peake, E. G. | Major | Royal Engineers | O.B.E. Mentioned in Despatches twice. |
| Redmond, Stephen | Gunner | Royal Horse Artillery | — |
| *Reddy, Francis | Corporal | 1st Yorks. and Lancs. Regiment | — |
| Robinet, Charles | Corporal | 3rd Royal Dublin Fusiliers | — |
| Roche, Cecil | 2nd Lieutenant | Royal Dublin Fusiliers | — |
| Ryan, Andrew | Guardsman | 1st Irish Guards | — |
| *Ryan, William | Guardsman | 1st Irish Guards | — |
| Scally, Edward | Sergeant | Leinster Regiment | — |
| Seddall, R. F. | Captain | Royal Army Service Corps (24th Divisional Train) | Mentioned in Despatches. |
| *Shiel, C. | Lieutenant | Royal Air Force | — |
| Shildrick, L. R. | Major | 2nd Royal Munsters | Mentioned in Despatches. |
| Shirley, Henry | Sergeant | Royal Army Medical Corps | — |
| *Sinclair, Alexander | Sergeant | 6th Connaught Rangers | — |
| Smyth, John | Guardsman | 1st Irish Guards | — |
| Somerfield, E. | Captain | 10th Royal Irish Rifles | — |
| *Stafford, Francis | Rifleman | 6th Royal Irish Rifles | — |
| Stafford, George | Private | 10th Royal Dublin Fusiliers | — |
| Stephens, Robert H. | Petty Officer, 1st class | Royal Naval Sick Berth Reserve | — |
| Switzer, Robert | Captain | 7th Royal Irish Regiment | Military Cross. Meritorious Service Medal. |
| Tait, William | 2nd Lieutenant | Tank Corps | — |
| Tanham, Bernard | Private | 6th Leinster Regiment | — |
| Thornton, J. J. | Chief Petty Officer. | Royal Naval Auxiliary Sick Berth Reserve | — |
| Toner, James | Sergeant | Royal Field Artillery | — |
| Turnbull, James A. | Private | Royal Army Medical Corps | — |
| Waugh, C. S. | Lieutenant | The King's Own Yorkshire Light Infantry | — |
| Weeks, O. H. | Captain | Royal Air Force | — |
| Wilson, George | Private | 10th Royal Dublin Fusiliers | — |
| Woods, George F. | Guardsman | 2nd Irish Guards | Distinguished Service Medal |

\* Killed in action or died of wounds.

### CASH OFFICE.

| NAME. | RANK. | REGIMENT. | DECORATION. |
|---|---|---|---|
| Johnson, R. S. | Lieutenant | 1st London Regt. (Roy.Fusiliers) | — |
| Jolley, W. E. | Sub-Lieutenant | Royal Naval Volunteer Reserve | — |

### CASK DEPARTMENT.

| NAME. | RANK. | REGIMENT. | DECORATION. |
|---|---|---|---|
| Allan, D. | Private | Royal Army Medical Corps | — |
| Dykes, R. | Lieutenant | 6th Black Watch (Royal Highlanders) | — |
| Giffin, W. C. D. | Lieutenant | 2nd Royal Irish Regiment | Distinguished Service Order. Military Cross. Mentioned in Despatches. |
| *Howard, George | Private | 10th Royal Dublin Fusiliers | — |
| Kerrigan, W. J. | Corporal | Royal Army Medical Corps | — |
| Mooney, R. T. | Acting-Corporal | 1st Royal Dublin Fusiliers | — |
| McAree, J. | Pioneer | Royal Engineers | — |
| Rawson, R. | Lance-Corporal | 10th Royal Dublin Fusiliers | — |
| Tyrrell, P. J. | Staff Sergeant | Royal Army Medical Corps | — |
| Walker, Henry | Corporal | Royal Army Medical Corps | — |
| Wallace, J. J. | Lieutenant | Royal Army Service Corps | — |
| *Yarnell, V. F. H. | Trooper | South Irish Horse | — |

### COOKE'S LANE MALTINGS.

| NAME. | RANK. | REGIMENT. | DECORATION. |
|---|---|---|---|
| Byrne, John | Lance-Corporal | 2nd Royal Welsh Fusiliers | — |
| Doonan, William | Guardsman | 1st Irish Guards | — |
| Hennessy, Thomas | Sergeant | 6th Dragoon Guards | — |
| *Holt, John H. | Private | 2/6th North Stafford Regiment | — |
| *Kennedy, James | Private | 1st Royal Dublin Fusiliers | — |
| Nolan, John | Guardsman | 2nd Irish Guards | — |
| Powderly, Christopher W. | Sergeant | 4th King's Own Liverpool Regt. | — |

\* Killed in action or died of wounds.

## Shell from World War I

"My uncle, John Graham, was in the Royal Navy during World War I. He was in the communications department on several battleships and he picked up this shell as a memento on one of those ships. It had been fired twice because there were markings on the back of it. After the war, he brought this home to his brother in Killeagh, Co. Cork. He came back to Ireland in ill-health and died shortly afterwards. His brother gave it to me over fifty years ago and I have kept it on the mantlepiece since then. It has appeared a few times in my grandchildren's school projects and I think it's an important symbol of Irish participation in World War I."

JOE MCCARTHY

## British Union Handkerchief

"This Union Jack flag belonged to my grandfather, David McClintock. It originates from when he fought and died in World War I. It is made of cotton and is hemmed all the way around and contains four expressions, 'Be Prepared,' 'Faithful to the Flag,' 'Defence not Defiance,' and 'Our King and Country'."

EVELYN KELLY

## Trench Art from World War I

"I remember my father used to take this object out from the cupboard and show it to my sister and me. It's a French wine bottle that was used to make trench art and it's an object that gives us an insight into my grandfather's activities during World War I. Our family knows very little about his time spent in the British Army. His name was Thomas St. John (b.1851, d.1951). He was a member of the Royal Irish Regiment and received an army pension up until his death. This item was made by him during his time fighting in France and he subsequently brought it home with him to Ireland. It's a cross, with a ladder fashioned inside a wine bottle and filled with gun oil. For us, this object is a fascinating piece of our family's history and is one of the few remaining physical links left by our grandfather that tells the story of his time spent fighting in the British Army during World War I."

JOHN ST JOHN

## Chinese Labour Corp Banner

"My grandfather, Jim Maultsaid, enlisted in the British Army in 1914. After injury in the Battle of the Somme, he was taken away from the field of battle. He recuperated and returned to service as acting captain of the 169 Company, Chinese Labour Corp in France. The Chinese Labour Corp comprised of over 96,000 Chinese workers who were largely recruited from the Shandong Province in China in 1917. These workers were contracted to do the logistics work in the closing stages of World War I, essentially running supply lines and then ultimately clearing up after the Armistice. This would involve clearing munitions, burying bodies, dismantling tanks and trains. This banner was created by members of the 169 Company and was presented to my grandfather at the end of his service with the Corp. To the best of our knowledge, it is unique insofar as no other officer was presented with anything like this and he took it as a very special gesture. The reason he was given it was because he treated members of the Company very well and with respect. Today, the people who worked as part of the Chinese Labour Corp are referred to as the, "The forgotten of the forgotten," as their role in the Great War has been largely marginalised. Fortunately, a monument in London is currently being created and my grandfather's words will be inscribed on the monument reading "Bravo, the boys from land of the dragon. Bravo indeed."

JOHN ROSBOROUGH

Part 1.
6d. Net.
The
GREAT·WAR
THE STANDARD HISTORY OF THE ALL-EUROPE CONFLICT
Edited by H.W. Wilson, author of
"With the Flag to Pretoria," "Japan's Fight for Freedom," etc.
(Photo: H. Walter Barnett.)

## The Great War– The Standard History of the All Europe Conflict

"This is the first issue of a magazine from the time of World War I. I think this magazine and others in the series were issued during the war to keep people informed as to what was going on. I have twelve of them and this one is the first in the series. My grandfather fought in World War I as part of the Royal Army Service Corp. When I saw these magazines in an antiques shop in Cork, I had to buy them as I find these items of great interest and importance for our history. You can pull up so much historical information on the internet nowadays, but I really love having old books and documents such as these in my possession where I can hold and enjoy them."

DAVID CUNNINGHAM

# Letter from King George V

"This is a letter my great-grandmother received from Buckingham Palace in 1918 when my great-grandfather was released as a prisoner of war in World War I. Private Isaac Byrne served with the Royal Dublin Fusiliers and the letter opens, 'The Queen joins me in welcoming you on your release from the miseries and hardships, which you have endured with so much patience and courage.' These letters were part of the first ever mass communication from a reigning British monarch and this letter was reproduced and distributed to all returning prisoners of war using lithography."

SEAN FRANCIS BYRNE

## 26 County Casualties of the Great War – 15 Volumes

"This 15 volume collection (published in 2017) is the updated version of Ireland's Memorial Records (published in 1923), but only for the 26 counties. I wrote and published it myself and it includes all the soldiers that are missing from Ireland's Memorial Records, including every mention of a casualty in any newspaper for the 26 counties. I have been researching and collecting all of this information for over 15 years. Nobody else was doing it and I felt it had to be done so I did it myself without any support. The approach I took was to draw on numerous resources, not just one resource. The result was that I was able to reveal almost twice as many Irish that died in wars than any other volume previously. It is my personal passion. I originally began by uncovering the death of a couple of lads from Holycross, Tipperary. I started there, then I did Thurles, then I did Tipperary County, then the whole thing stretched out and I couldn't stop until I did the 26 counties. I have been unemployed for over 10 years and it has been difficult to assemble this all by myself, but I did it, all 22kg of it, all 9,000 pages, every one of the eight million words in it. While creating this, I have had 30,000 soldiers looking over my shoulder, urging me on, and I'm very proud of it. In many ways, it's an on-going project because new deaths from the Great War are still being uncovered."

TOM BURNELL

## Macroom
## Hooded Cloak

"My husband's grandfather was a
master tailor by the name of Patrick
Cunningham from Cork Street,
Macroom, Co. Cork. He made this
hooded cloak for his wife, Hannora
Desmond, Kilmurry, Co. Cork . It was
subsequently worn by their daughter,
Nora Cunningham. She was a prominent
member of Cumann na mBan from 1914
–1923 (her sister Molly was president of
Macroom Cumann na mBan) and would
have hidden guns under the cloak. The
cloak was worn by Nora during the 1916
Rising whilst intelligence gathering
and running guns and medical supplies
to 7th Battalion, 1st Cork Brigade
(Macroom). That brigade rose during
Easter Week to march from Macroom
to Banna Strand in Co. Kerry, but only
reached Carriganima Co Cork where
they had to abandon the march. In this
cloak, Nora would have brought the
message that Roger Casement had been
captured and that the battalion had to
return to Macroom. Nora continued to
be active up to and during the War of
Independence. She would continue to
carry guns and ammunitions concealed
under this cloak. She was later searched
by the RIC, arrested, and taken to
Macroom Castle. An order was issued
that she was barred from the town and
was to be shot on sight. She continued
her activities by swimming at night
up the Sullane River from Doonisky to
Macroom. If the river was flooded, she
would walk along the railway line,
but this was more dangerous for her
as she could have been easily spotted
by the R.I.C."

CATHY ARMSTRONG

## 1918 Prison Uniform

"This is a prison uniform belonging to my grandfather (also Thomas Barrett) who was very active in the Galway area during the 1916 Rising. He spent time in a number of prisons in Ireland and the UK. For years, the story in my family was that he had escaped from prison with the uniform, but we have recently researched it and we now know that he smuggled it out upon his release. The uniform is a really important part of our family history but also tells a piece of Ireland's story during those turbulent times."

**THOMAS BARRETT**

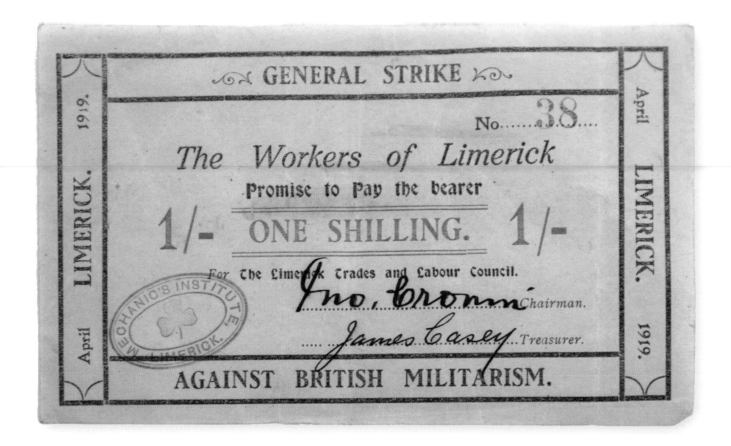

## Limerick Soviet Currency

"This note was produced during the general strike in Limerick in 1919, commonly known as the Limerick Soviet. It is one of several notes of different denominations we hold as a family. One of the signatories on these notes is my great grandfather John Cronin who was leader of the Limerick Soviet campaign. He was the head of the Carpenters Union in Limerick at the time and that's how he got involved in the Soviet. He was a renowned carpenter and his work can still be seen around Limerick today, including the confessional boxes in St. Saviour's Church."

GERRY CASEY

## A Historic Quilt Relating to the Anglican Church

"In the Magheragall Parish, County Antrim, there is evidence that people made quilts in which you paid to have your name added to a quilt and then the quilt was auctioned. This is an example that survived. It is red in colour with a centre piece that reads 'GOD SAVE THE QUEEN'. It was pre-partition at the time so it has a HARP in the very centre, a symbol that would have fallen into disuse in the area after partition I think. Interestingly, Magheragall is also the home church of Ernest Blythe, his parents are buried here."

NICHOLAS DARK

## Strut from the First Airplane to Complete a Transatlantic Flight

"This is a strut from the Vickers Vimy plane that took part in the first transatlantic flight that crash landed in Clifden, Co. Galway on the 15th of June, 1919. It was a huge moment in Irish history and was a truly global news event at the time. The two men who flew the plane were called Alcock and Brown and because of this flight, this plane is one of the most important in aviation history.

As a young man, I purchased this object when the opportunity arose. I was into history and up to that stage I had been collecting dinky toys all my life. I had a number of tea chests full of them and when this strut came in front of me, it was a natural progression, so I saved and purchased it. Subsequently, my father got rid of the tea chests with the dinky toys (he said I was too big for them), but I held on to the strut."

EUGENE EGAN

## A Belt from Frongoch

"My grandfather, Seamus Ó Chaomhanaigh, was Officer Commanding of Óglaigh na hÉireann in Derry in 1916. After the events of 1916, republicans and republican sympathisers all across Ireland were interned by the British, including my grandfather. They were sent to Frongoch internment camp and to pass the time, the republicans produced many handcrafts (harps, Celtic crosses, etc.). Seamus made this belt while he was there. On the belt, it reads "Seachtain na Cásga," meaning Easter Week. Alongside the text, are two flags: the Irish tricolour and the flag of the Transvaal Republic in Southern Africa. During the Boer War, Seamus was in the British Army. He saw first-hand the treatment the British dished out to the Boers and the presence of the Transvaal flag (one of the Boer republics) on this belt shows how that experience changed his world view. He later participated in the War of Independence and was arrested in April 1920 in Derry. He was subsequently sent to Wormwood Scrubs in London where he joined a hunger strike. Seamus was eventually released in a state of collapse to St James' nursing home in London. Throughout this period, he still had the belt with him and the photo of him in the nursing home shows him convalescing with the belt on his lap. This belt is very important to our family and has been in our possession ever since."

COLM Ó TUATHALÁIN

## Cigarette Box

"This is a silver cigarette box that saved my maternal great-grandfather's life. His name was Macca Powell, and he was the CEO of Mangan Jewellers in Saint Patrick's Street, Cork. In 1920, my great-grandfather was chased though the store by the Black and Tans. He was shot at by them, and at one stage they shot at his heart, but he had a silver cigarette box inside his waistcoat, and the bullets hit the box instead of him and saved his life. A rare case where cigarettes are good for you! I'm also holding a picture of Macca's grandson, Ronnie (my father), on the roof garden of Mangan's where he lived up to the age of 10 years."

BILL SMITH

## War of Independence Grenade

"This grenade was made in a secret bunker in Knockraha near Watergrasshill, Co. Cork in a mould that was produced surreptitiously in the Ford factory in Cork City. In 1918, employees of the factory sympathetic to the IRA's cause, secretly produced the moulds using the materials and skills that were available to them in the manufacturing plant. The moulds were then taken to a secret location and live grenades were produced from them for use in the war. This grenade that I have in my possession was most likely a dud. It was embedded in the pillar of the gate to the parochial house in Watergrasshill until the 1970s when my friend dug it out. I've had it ever since. The moulds are owned by a local man called Jim Fitzgerald who inherited them directly from some former IRA members."

BARRY CURTIN

## Colt 45 Gun

"This Colt 45 gun belonged to my grand-uncle, Mick Hynes. Mick joined the IRA as a teenager and was involved in guerrilla warfare against the British. Eventually he was caught and tried, sent to Pentonville Prison, and subsequently died there. While the reason for his death is unclear from the death certificate, my family believed it was due to maltreatment. This gun was used before the Civil War, and when he went on the run, he gave it to his sister, May, to look after. It is part of my family story and a big part of who we are."

ALISON KILLILEA

## Bowler Hat

"This is my great-grandfather's bowler hat. He was born in 1892 and served in Michael Collins' Army during the Civil War. At that time, his future wife was serving on the opposite side as a runner for Éamon de Valera. She was arrested and was brought to prison in Tralee. My great-grandfather was working as a guard in the prison and he met her when he was bringing her food. Even though they were from either side of the divide, they fell in love. When she was released, they married and, from 1927, he ran a draper shop on the Western Road in Clonakilty. It would have been a great sign of wealth having a bowler hat and a cane. He was really into hats and there are plenty of pictures of him in suits as well. After he died in 1944, the hat was stored in the house. It was found two years ago after my grand-uncle, Pat, passed away. My great-grandfather's name is on the inside: C. Fitz Clon (Cornelius Fitzpatrick)."

JAMES KIELY

## Civil War Prisoner Art

"These objects were created by a republican prisoner called William O'Mahony while incarcerated in Cork Gaol during the Civil War in 1922. Included are a Celtic Cross constructed of matchsticks and broken glass, a Crucifix made of .303 rifle bullet cases, and a hand-painted replica of the Irish Proclamation. William gave them to my father's cousin, Madge Walsh, in the 1920s in recognition of her role in Cumann na mBan during the War of Independence. She lived in Tivoli in Cork City and I met her once or twice when I was a child in the late 1970s. I don't know much about her exploits during the war, but I imagine she was quite active given that she was gifted these specially created items."

CONOR KELLEHER

## Key to the Old Cork City Gaol

"These are a complete set of keys to the Old Cork City Gaol that stood on the current site of University College Cork. I purchased the keys from a friend of mine, a Mr Dan Driscoll, who worked as a young man digging trenches when the prison was being demolished and foundations were being laid for an extension to the university. Dan was working in the trench with a pick and shovel when a lorry driver was loading a large safe on to the back of a truck. The safe fell and the keys fell out on to the ground. The driver of the truck picked up the keys and threw them to Dan and shouted, "You might want to get out of here some day!" I collect many historical artefacts, but these keys are especially important to me as my father was imprisoned there during the Civil War."

DAVID WILLIS

## Rosary Beads

"These are my grandmother's rosary beads, but were handed down to her from generations before. I believe they are a distinctly Galway version of rosary beads. These are made out of hard fruit wood and silver. The cross is unusually tubular in shape, decorated with multi-colour string braids through the tube. The rosary is worn with use, with the owner feeling one's way along the beads as you said the rosary. The fruit balls indicate that you say one 'Hail Mary' each, the silver balls indicate a decade of 'Hail Marys' and one 'Our Father'. It would have been in daily use. It has been in the family so long and it's a reminder of both my grandmother and my father."

PETER CONNOLLY

## An American Bus Chair

"My great-grandfather, John James Sloane, was born in Loch Gowna, Co. Cavan in the 1880s, but emigrated to the USA in early 1900s. There, he worked with the Fifth Avenue Coach Company as a bus driver (an attached picture shows him on one such bus). His father became ill about 1914, which forced John to return to Ireland to take over the running of the family farm and flax mill. Returning to Ireland, he brought back one of the bus seats from New York and had it made into a chair that he used for the rest of his life (he's pictured sitting on it in the family home, beside his wife). Today it is in a sorry state, but I look at it as a piece of well-loved and well-used furniture and a symbol that some of the diaspora did return."

NIALL SLOANE

## Breast Pump Made by Fannin & Co.

"This Irish-made breast pump for expressing milk was given to me by my grandmother whose babies were born between 1921 and 1931. This object reduced the discomfort that women experienced while breastfeeding and changed daily lives at the time considerably. In those days, women would have been weaker after childbirth and this object gave them an opportunity to breastfeed without too much physical effort. Someone else could even feed the baby with the expressed milk. I was a midwife and I tried to donate this object to various maternity hospitals hoping that they would have an archive but I never got a reply. Many people today are surprised to find out that breast pumps existed so long ago and I think it's important to realise now what it was like for women when the first breast pumps became available in Ireland."

EITHNE
LYNCH

## A Peat Postcard

"This is like a hen's tooth; it's a very rare postcard, exactly like any other postcard, except that it's made from peat moss. It was made in Kildare. The peat came from the Curragh to a mill in Celbridge, then they froze it, mixed it with chemicals, and made the postcards. Unfortunately, the process was so expensive that they went out of business after two years. How it came into my father's possession is a bit of mystery but we used to live directly across the road from the house that this postcard is addressed to."

MICHAEL DOYLE

## Sextant

"This is my grandfather's sextant. His name was Captain Michael Good originally from Fairhill in Cork City. He was a sea captain and, during his working life, he worked for P&O, the British Merchant Navy, and the British Tanker Company (now known as BP). He was on the sea through both World Wars and his father, a quarter-master with the City of Cork Steam Packet, was killed by a U-Boat in 1917. This sextant travelled with him all around the world, visiting Persia, India, and Italy. He never spoke much about his travels during war-time at home. During World War II, he wasn't home for two years. Afterwards, all his medals for participation in both wars were hidden but the sextant was not. It was originally calibrated in December 1925 and he used it for navigation to line up the stars and the horizon."

BRIAN WISEMAN

## Miner's Lamp

"This is my great-granduncle, James Fitzpatrick's miners lamp used in Castlecomer Coal Mines circa 1920s."

RONAN MIDDLETON

## A Razor to America and Back

"As a note written by my father, Paddy Murphy (RIP), on the 30th of June 1972 explains, this Crown & Sword cut-throat razor and a bar of soap was given to a neighbour's son in 1914 by my grandfather as a leaving present. Dan Fleming, then aged 20, was emigrating to America. Fifty-eight years later, after working as a policeman in America, Dan returned to his native Scartaglin, Co. Kerry, on holidays in June 1972 for the very first time since leaving. While back, Dan passed on the razor that had served him well to my father along with half a bar of the original soap. Sadly, the soap hasn't survived! This story is special to me because I feel it captures the friendship and good nature of village life in early 20th century rural Ireland and it also documents the story of emigration that was so prevalent throughout the country at that time."

MARGARET JACKMAN

## Guinness Cooper Cert

"This is my grandfather's certificate of admission to the Dublin Operative Coopers Society, alongside his coopers bowler hat, which they used to wear for ceremonial purposes. The skilled coopers were the barrel maker craftsmen in Guinness, and the society was akin to a brotherhood. He, like his father, my father, and my uncles (his sons), worked in Guinness all of their working lives – three generations. My father, Louis Hogan, worked in Guinness for 46 years from the age of 14, and was part of the team who introduced the aluminium cask, ending the barrel-making tradition. I have a tape recording of my father talking about that change. His job was to look at the efficiency of Guinness distribution around the country. Guinness decided to move from wooden barrels to aluminium casks so they could be loaded and distributed easier. Guinness is a huge part of our family's history and these objects remind us of a craft from yesteryear."

RONAN HOGAN

## Hooks from the Lagan in Lisburn

"These hooks came from my father-in-law. His father, Robert Blakely, was from Hilden, Lisburn and worked on the coal barges on the Lagan when he was young. They would attach these hooks to bamboo and drag it along. They used these hooks to pull up bodies from the river, apparently there were an awful lot in those days."

GEORGINA BLAKELY

## Muffin the Mule Marionette

"Muffin the Mule was a very famous puppet from the 1930s to 1950s. He was made popular on a British children's television show called, 'Here Comes Muffin'. Ann Hogarth and Jann Bussell designed the marionette and worked on the television series. I love this puppet and have had it all my life. I inherited it from my older sister and he has followed me around all my life. Back in the day, my Dad worked the puppet regularly and he was brilliant at pulling the strings and bringing Muffin to life. My mother was a pianist and she bought me the song book. I used to sing the theme song with my sister while my father worked the puppet at the same time. This puppet is very evocative of that time in my life. I still have the song book and I still play the song, but I can never work the puppet as well as my Dad."

CAROLE CULLEN

## Blue Hussars
## Model Soldiers

"This is one of very few model sets made of Irish military units post-Independence. They are lead models of the Blue Hussars who were the Irish Presidential Escort from 1932 until 1948 when they were disbanded. One of the first times the unit was used was during the Eucharistic Congress. The Irish government eventually got rid of them because they looked too imperial, a visual trapping maybe from when the British were here. They decided that it would better represent a modern state if the presidential escort rode motorbikes. This unit became the Motorcycle Unit (Second Cavalry Squadron) of the Cavalry Corps, although the name the Blue Hussars is still sometimes used to refer to them."

FERGAL BROWNE

## Garastún Árd-Oifig an Phoist, 1916

"This is a long rectangular photograph taken in 1938 with the members of the GPO garrison from the Easter Rising of 1916. It shows the women and the men who were actually in the GPO. It was taken by an *Irish Press* photographer against the railway end of Croke Park. My grandfather, P.J. McGrath, and his son, Paddy McGrath, are both in the photograph. They were involved in the fighting in the GPO together and Paddy was injured on the roof, despite his father telling him not to go up there. After 1916, William Martin Murphy, proprietor of the *Irish Independent* and owner of the Dublin Tramway Company, helped free my grandfather from prison as P.J. had earlier saved Murphy's life during the 1913 Lockout whilst working in the *Independent*. His son, Paddy, was sent to hospital after the Rising. Fortunately for him, the nurse in the hospital changed his date of birth to 16 so he was released immediately but his injury affected him throughout his life."

BRIAN DERMODY

## Official Handbook of the Irish Free State

"This is a copy of the first official handbook of the Irish Free State that was published in 1932. It was created by a committee established by the government at the time and is in essence an encyclopaedia of the state covering different topics. The committee decided on all the chapters, including topics like, 'the country and its people', 'flora and fauna', 'folklore', and there is also reference information, such as details of Irish consulates around the world. There is also a beautiful large fold-out map included, which I particularly like. This copy is a family heirloom and my uncle's name is written on the inside. He was a teacher and would have bought the book new. I have dipped into it over the years when looking for various pieces of information. For me, it's an item to be cherished because it holds up a mirror to the country at the foundation of the state."

DAVID WALSH

## Spring Show Poster 1936

"This is a mounted original poster from the RDS Spring Show of 1936 showing a very colourful woman, probably Hibernia, surrounded by a generous harvest of fruits and vegetables in an art deco style. I found it in an antiques store in Miami and I had to buy it and bring it home."

ADRIENNE FERGUSON

## The Bones of St. Peter and St. Paul

"My father had three brothers who were all priests. One of them, Monsignor John Power, was well connected in the Vatican. He was given these bones in 1933 by Monsignor Parolin, Anna Sarto's nephew. Anna was the sister of Pope Pius X. The bones were first presented by Cardinal Cavallari to Pope Pius X (Giuseppe Sarto) on the occasion of his jubilee in 1908. He bequeathed them to his sisters, Anna and Maria, when he died in 1914 but they stayed in the possession of two of Pope Pius X's successors (Pope Benedict XV and Pope Pius XI), until Pope Pius XI returned them to the Sarto sisters in 1924. When Anna Sarto died in 1930, she left the bones to her nephew, Monsignor Parolin. In 1933, Monsignor Parolin left them to my uncle, Monsignor (then Fr.) John Power. As a friend of Monsignor Parolin, my uncle also knew and was in regular contact with Pope Pius X's grand-niece, Maria Sarto. My uncle had organised the funding for a church to be built in his then parish in Saltley, Birmingham and so he brought the relics to England where they were venerated in the Church of the Holy Rosary. During World War II, he thought that the relics would be safer in Ireland, where my father and mother lived. He asked the then Taoiseach, De Valera, to personally mind them in his home in Booterstown, Dublin. After the war, De Valera returned them to my mother and father. When I was born in 1935, my uncle Monsignor John Power, asked Maria Sarto to be my godmother. She had no children of her own. She couldn't attend my christening but we wrote to each other over the years and I met her for the first time in Rome in 1950, when she and my uncle bequeathed the relics to me. I also have in my possession an official letter from the Vatican confirming that the bones are the true relics of St. Peter and St. Paul."

MARY THÉRÈSE GALVIN

## Widow's Weed

"Historically, death has had many customs. Clocks were stopped, mirrors covered, windows opened. Women who had helped with childbirth would also be those who would bring embroidered linen sheets to lay the deceased out on. The poorer people's sheets were often 10 stone Morton's flour bags (Ballymena), the famous blackbird logo having been bleached out. Pre war, Catholic coffins were covered in brown cloth, Protestant coffins in black cloth. Up until the 17th century, the dead could only wear woollen shrouds in England (protecting the wool trade). Mourners were issued black armbands or black cloth diamonds. Handkerchiefs had black edges. The clergyman wore a white silk scarf as did the undertaker, with a white ribbon on his top hat if the deceased was a woman. Sometimes invitation cards were sent to friends with the time and place of the funeral. The Victorian era had a morbid indulgence in everything draped or clothed in black. The widow's weeds I am wearing was the fashion following Queen Victoria after her husband Albert's death. She wore a similar headdress at his funeral. This one belonged to a Mrs Boyd, grandmother to the McKinley sisters from Broughshane, Co. Antrim."

**BETTY SHAW**

## A Burial Habit

"This is a burial habit that was one of many items given to my daughter Sharon Whooley, by Tony McCarthy from Inishannon, Co. Cork. His family had a drapery shop, Murphy's in Mallow, and were in business for over seventy years, from the 1920s to the 1990s. Ellen Murphy was also a milliner and many examples of her exquisite work still remains. Her son, Bertie, started in the shop in the early 1940s when he was just sixteen and eventually took over. The family were careful and never threw out a single item of unsold stock: pure wool coats, corsets, communion dresses, bridal veils, and silk stockings, all 'Déanta in Éireann'. What remains is a treasure trove; a time capsule, of everyday life in a small town in Ireland, how people lived and how people died."

SALLY DALY

## Overbecks Rejuvenator

"This is an electronic panacea device, including an instruction booklet explaining how to apply electrodes to various parts of the body to cure ailments through conducting electric currents. I took a course to become a cardiac first responder and when I discovered this recently in a friend's house

after the course, it caught my eye. In some ways, it's sort of the fore-runner of a defibrillator. Personally, I'd be nervous about using it and the battery has long since disappeared anyway."

MARY MULLIGAN

# 1943 Belfast Celtic Jersey

"This is Paddy Bonnar's Belfast Celtic shirt from 1943. Belfast Celtic was one of the most successful teams in Irish soccer until they withdrew from the league in 1949. For both west and south Belfast, this club was the biggest football team ever. Paddy played on the wing and he had an aim like a ballistic missile. The team was not sectarian. Its players came from both sides of the community. Its most famous manager, Elisha Scott, was a Protestant. The club left the league in controversial circumstances in 1949. One of their players, Jimmy Jones, had been attacked by rival fans after the derby match with Linfield on St. Stephen's Day, 1948. The Irish Football Association's failure to issue an appropriate punishment for Linfield incensed the Celtic board who voted to resign from the league. However, before making that decision public, the club's best players were sold to English teams. Bonnar transferred to Aldershot. On April 22nd, 1949, as the club prepared to travel to Cobh to embark on a pre-arranged tour to America and Canada, a letter of resignation was sent to the Irish FA. The football authorities had no time to respond. Belfast Celtic never played a league match again."

JOHN BOYLE
AND HEIDI BOYLE
(NÉE BONNAR)

## Patchwork Quilt

"This patchwork quilt has been handed down in our family through the generations. It is a wedding quilt and was passed from daughter to daughter as a dowry and then on to a daughter-in-law. The quilt originates from 1858 and was originally created by Ellen Buttimer from Dunmanway. Since then, every generation has added to the quilt or has had patches repaired. It is now our turn to safeguard the quilt and we will eventually give it to our daughter. It is so special for us because it has so much love in it, so much feeling, and so much creativity. It has existed for so long, and even though it has been well used, it is still beautiful."

NOEL & MELODY BUCKLEY

## Seed Fiddle

"This seed fiddle belonged to my father, and it was used to plant the flax to make cotton. It's a rare gadget that was used to spread the seed. You wear it on your shoulder and it has a body where you put the seed that falls into a plate, which rolls when you pull and push the bow along the front of it, spreading the seed. There used to be flax mills all across West Cork and farmers used to be on contract to the mills, including my father. I remember when we all built our new houses, he used the seed fiddle to set the lawns. It was perfect for the job. My father passed away a number of years ago. Throughout my life, this object has always been there and now when I see it, it reminds me of him."

JEREMIAH O'SULLIVAN

## Luftwaffe Officer Dagger

"My grandfather fought in World War II and somehow survived the entire war. As a child, I always asked him about the war, but understandably he didn't like to talk about it. He did, however, write letters detailing his time in the war and when he died, he left me this dagger, which he took from a German officer who was killed. My grandfather died a number of years ago at the age of 90, but this dagger keeps me connected to him. Every time I look at it, I think of him and the great man he was."

PAUL HEFFERNAN

## Bullet Shrine

"This bullet shrine, with a miniature figure of St. Anthony of Padua inside, was my mother's. The bullet has been carved to house the figure and can rotate to ensure the saint remains safely inside. Such bullet shrines were carried in soldiers' pockets during the First and Second World Wars. We suspect a soldier, probably a patient, gave it to my mother when she worked in St Guy's Hospital in London in the 1940s, one of the Military and War hospitals in the UK. She always kept it safe and 'minded it' through the years. It not only reminds me of her, but particularly when she was young and how life must have seemed to her then as a young nurse in London in her very early 20s. It also strikes me as a contradictory object of war/killing being used for devotion, a juxtaposition of sorts between two objects (the bullet and the saintly figurine), between war and peace. The object therefore is representative of those times in Ireland in the 1940s and certainly also wider Europe. To my mother, perhaps it reminded her too of the patient who fought and who she met in her youth."

CONNIE KELLEHER

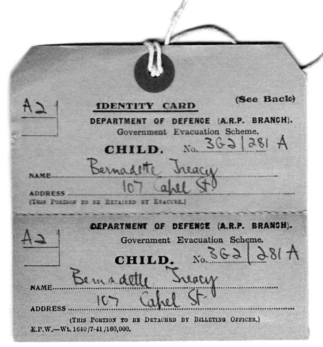

## Evacuation Card

"This is the evacuation card I received during World War II shortly after my birth in Dublin. Also sent was a cover letter with the identity card. At the time, we lived in Capel Street and there were plans afoot for evacuating Dublin children, similar to what was happening in Britain at the time. When I recently uncovered it in my mother's possessions, I thought it was a bit of history. We never knew anything about it, but during the war, it must have looked like Ireland was going to be badly affected, and in some ways it was, as happened with the North Strand bombing."

BERNADETTE FOLEY

## 1943 Gas Mask

"This is a children's gas mask issued during World War II by the Irish government. My mother, Delia, had to go and to pick up seven gas masks for herself and the family, including one for me, in case of bombing. I was five years old at the time. The gas mask was never used and is marked as 'small'. It's in an original box with leaflets and identity cards. It's a good job that we didn't have to use them because I believe the gas masks were filled with asbestos and would probably have killed us before the bombs did."

PADDY O'DONOGHUE

## Door Knocker from the Old Galway Gaol

"This is an iron door knocker in the shape of a horseshoe with a lion's head in the centre and a hand holding the top of the knocker. James Rice, my father, was part of the demolition team of the old Galway Gaol. The hand at the top of the knocker now has painted red nails and I believe this was done by one of my daughters. There is now a cathedral where the Gaol stood and this knocker is one of the last remnants of the building."

MICHAEL RICE

# Rabbit Trap

"My father, John Mc Hugh, trapped rabbits during World War II in Portnoo, Co Donegal, and dispatched them to Dublin from Glenties Railway Station, which is now long closed. I think that they were then sent to England. It was extremely hard work setting traps and collecting rabbits every day in all weathers. There were no quads then and everything had to be carried. He had to pay rent to landowners to trap on their property and he was bringing up a family with no unemployment support. He saved enough money from a number of years doing this to be able to buy the first new Massey Ferguson tractor in the Parish of Ardara, from McMahons in Milford for 350 pounds and bought 15 more during his working life. That first machine he bought changed lives in the whole area and he achieved it from virtually nothing. He suffered badly from arthritis, probably from all the wetness when trapping."

GERALD MCHUGH

## Jewish Tallith Shawl

"This is my grandfather's Tallith, his prayer shawl, that he should have been buried in according to Jewish custom. Instead, he met with death, when he was gassed in Auschwitz, the concentration camp run by the Nazi regime. My father, the poet, Maurits Mok, somehow smuggled it at great risk, as he was a persecuted Jew himself, through World War II while hiding in different places every six weeks. I knew it as a barcode of memory pinned to his wall and when my father died, it travelled with me through Europe to all the different countries I lived in before I ended up in Ireland. Here it rests beside my desk and I stroke it sometimes, thinking or imagining that my grandfather would have loved all the places that his prayer shawl has been brought to. It is all I have from my grandfather."

JUDITH MOK

## Quilt Made in England Using Fabric Samples

"My great-aunts Mary (May) and Hannah (Bob) O'Neill emigrated to Essex from Tipperary in the 1940s and spent all their working lives nursing in England. At some point during this time, they were tasked with organising the replacement of curtains in the hospital wards they worked in. This involved gathering many fabric sample books. After they replaced the hospital curtains, they took the sample books home and set about making this quilt. The front of the quilt, as you can see, is created from various samples and the reverse is actually made from some of the old curtains that had been taken down in the ward. Neither of the women married and when they came home from England after retirement, they brought the quilt and it remained in their house until Hannah's death five years ago when I inherited it. I have a real interest in women's history and craftwork. I love this item as it represents the hundreds of Irish women who went abroad to work in nursing. Their thrift and artistry, skills, and the determination required to create something as beautiful and functional as this is evident in this piece."

EILÍS NIC DHONNCHA

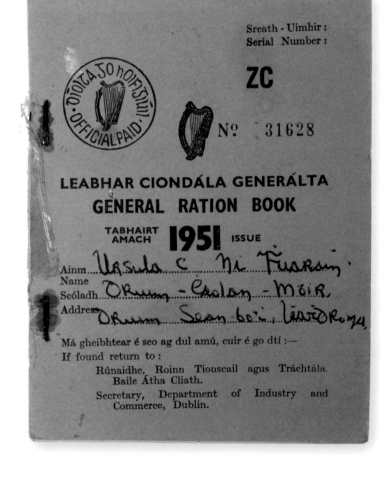

## Ration Book

"This iconic ration book is important to me as I was five years old when it was issued to me in 1951 so I could not have been aware of the conditions of the time. It is unused, which points to improving circumstances and perhaps even honesty on my parents part: they did not, could not perhaps, use it for themselves or swap some of its coupons for other ones. The ration book is an emblem of a time long passed in Ireland but a reminder of the suffering that war brought to our neutral country. In 1951, the United Nations was in its infancy, the European Union was still a long way off, and the idea of relief agencies hardly conceived. Our self-reliant government endeavoured to feed its people."

URSULA FORAN

## Volcano Kettle

"This volcano kettle belonged to
my grandmother in the 1950s. She
lived in Claremorris, Co. Mayo where
she may have bought it. She spent
many holidays on Achill Island so she
could have bought it in Sweeney's
of Achill either. I inherited it as I do
a lot of camping. The volcano kettle
has once again become popular
(made by Kellys) for campers
as it is very efficient and
environmentally friendly.
The idea behind it is that
only a small few twigs or
pine cones are needed
to quickly boil water.
My grandmother loved
all things Mayo and
she encouraged us all
to holiday on Achill.
She kept outdoor living
going in our family with
camping etc. and this
object represents that. It
is a family heirloom and
will continue to be passed
on to future generations."

LIZ MCMAHON

## All-Ireland Antrim Camogie Winners Collection

"This is a collection of items relating to my mummy, Marion McFetridge (née Kearns) who played forward for the Antrim Camogie Team from the age of 14 to 33. It includes two All-Ireland medals (1956 & 1967), eight Inter-provincial medals, and a 1967 All-Ireland winning plaque. In 1956 she scored 2 goals against Cork that ended the run of 18 successive All-Irelands for Dublin, at 17 years of age she was named Antrim All-star, in 1967 she scored 3 goals in the replay against Dublin that stopped their 10-in-a-row campaign, and in 2009 she was named in the 'Ulster Team of the Century'. She often said that being a GAA player was an invaluable calling card in many counties, it also afforded her the opportunity to see Ireland and make life-long friends. From her love of the GAA she instilled in her three daughters a healthy competitiveness, respect, a love of sport, deeply held loyalty and, the ability to grab life by the horns whilst living in the moment. Her obsession with the GAA even meant that she would insist on visiting the county who won the hurling and football as soon after the All-Ireland finals as possible – so she could join in the craic! At mummy's funeral in March 2017, GAA people came from all over Ireland to pay their respects determined to let us know what a remarkable women she was. She would be so proud to showcase these items as part of National Treasures to show what a positive role camogie and the GAA played in her life growing up in the north of Ireland."

PAULA MCFETRIDGE

## Gaelic Football from 1958 Kerry Minor County Final

"This ball was used in the 1958 Kerry GAA minor football club championship final and the match was won by Tralee's John Mitchel's Club. My late father, Michael Jacques McDonnell, was the team trainer and I was the team mascot. He painted the ball in the team's colours of green and gold with each of the player's names inscribed in Irish. Throughout his life, my father documented everything and this ball became an important keepsake of that win. My grand-daughter, Ciara Harris, is playing for John Mitchel's Club today."

JOE MCDONNELL

## Aer Lingus Poster Original Artwork

"A snapshot back to a time when Aer Lingus and the state in general were exploring new ways of expressing and promoting their identity in the context of travel and tourism. My father, Jan de Fouw, was one of a number of young Dutch designers, new to Ireland who helped to explore this new image through his graphic work. My father donated many of his original artworks to the National Irish Visual Arts Library in IADT, but there are still a number of original hand-painted poster designs on cardboard, like these, in the family's possession."

REMCO DE FOUW

## Frank Aiken's Aer Lingus Bag

"This bag belonged to my father, the politician and Minister of External Affairs, Frank Aiken. He wrote his initials, PMcA in Irish in small writing in pencil on the front of the bag. He travelled to the United Nations in New York in the late 1950s and 1960s and always flew with Aer Lingus. He was instrumental in setting up the national airline and carried this bag proudly, using it to hold his personal belongings."

FRANK AIKEN

## Box Made in TB Sanatorium

"This item was made by my mother, Elizabeth Walsh Glynn, in Peamount Hospital, Newcastle, Co. Dublin in the 1940s. She was from Co. Wexford and spent three years in the hospital due to the tuberculosis epidemic at the time. My eldest sister was born there too. Looking back, she was lucky to have survived as it wasn't until the 1950s that a cure for tuberculosis became readily available in Ireland. The patients had to spend the majority of their time lying flat and would have been up on their feet for only a few hours each evening. During this time, they engaged in crafts to keep them busy and to stave off the boredom. This box was hand-woven by her during her recovery time and displays various pictures of cottages on all sides. My mother loved gardening and this explains why she would have chosen the garden images on the box. The plastic laminate over the top of the box is from

recycled X-rays that the doctors provided. Interestingly, my mother and my siblings always referred to this item as a casket rather than a box. Everything about the object is original and maintained and it has become a valuable part of our family's history."

DOLORES KELLY

## Unopened Easter Egg from 1959

"My grandmother, Eileen Dignam, bought this Easter egg in 1959 with the intention of giving it to her daughter, Olive. Olive was in hospital at the time suffering from consumption and sadly she died three weeks before Easter. My granny kept it until her death in 1993, as she didn't have the heart to throw it away. I have kept it since then in memory of my aunt."

TERRY GOLDSMITH

## Mayo Abú

"This hat was bought in the 1970s on my way to a GAA football match to support my home county Mayo on their mission to get the Sam Maguire Cup back. I bought it on Dublin's Dorset Street or perhaps the North Circular Road. At the time, there was a tradition where locals in that part of Dublin would get old cardboard boxes, perhaps Kellogg's cereal boxes, and paper maché to make hats to sell to the crowds going to Croke Park. I still wear this hat today but only to All-Ireland finals in memory of my father. He never witnessed a Mayo All-Ireland final, he was either too poor, too far away and eventually too old. In 2016, I was trudging home along the North Circular Road after a Mayo loss when I was stopped by some locals. They couldn't believe that one of the hats was still going, they took a photo of me and told me that their Mum used to make the hats. I am sure this hat will be there when Mayo win Sam again, even if I'm not."

JIM NEARY

## Mayo All-Ireland Programmes 1950 and 1951

"Our father, Peter McGing, was a die-hard Mayo fan, a young Garda 'exiled' in Dublin in the 1940s and 1950s! We grew up listening to great stories and blow by blow accounts of the two wonderful winning All-Irelands he attended as a young man. Then he waited for the next one. Alas, he died at 90 in 2013 without that luxury. Every year, he said, 'This will be our year!' After his death, we were clearing the attic of our family home in Clane, Co. Kildare when we found decades of memories, including these two gems: the programmes of those two All-Irelands Mayo won. They are complete with handwritten notes of every score and even an explanation that he borrowed a car to return early from holidays in Mayo to attend. We had never seen them before as they were stored in a 'safe place' during one of many house moves, prior to his suffering from dementia in later years. They are a treasure to us as they keep his memory burning brightly, and sum him up perfectly! And, of course, this year will be our year."

BREDA MCHALE

## Rabbit Named Janet

"This is my rabbit, Janet, who was made in the Tri-ang Factory on the Castlereagh Road in Belfast where two of my sisters worked. Amy worked in the factory and Phil worked in the office. I received Janet from Father Christmas in 1956 and she has stayed with me until recently when she was put into storage while I was renovating my house. Unfortunately, while she was there, she was damaged by mice. She was then put in the barn at my friend Felicity's house and I was going to finally abandon her, but Felicity kindly rescued and restored her and now she's back where she belongs. Janet now lives in my guest bedroom and my granddaughter, Noomi-Belle, loves to play with her when she comes to visit."

NORMA DOYLE

## Woolworths Medal

"My Aunt Nora was a floor manager, or a "floor walker" as they said, in the Woolworths shop on Cork's Saint Patrick's Street. She worked there all her life and received this medal for 21 years of service in the shop. Woolworths is long gone but it was one of the biggest shops in Cork at the time, selling a variety of miscellaneous items. I remember visiting the shop as a child and it had everything, from a needle to a haystack! They had a haberdashery and sweets all along the side of the shop where you could get a dolly mixture, clove rocks, cough sweets, everything. I have held on to this object because Woolworths was such a great institution. I don't think we will see too many medals given out to employees for 21 years of service anymore given how employment has changed, so this is a real treasure."

JOE MURRAY

## Cookery Apron, Cookery Book, Shield, Sash with County Name

"A collection of items, including a shield (National Bread Baking Competition, 1968), sash, apron, and cookery book from the occasion of the national final of the schools' bread baking competition held in the Abbey Theatre, Dublin on the 8th of December, 1968. Longford came first, Galway second, and Waterford came third. All contestants were given an electric hair dryer and a cheque to cover costs, as the event was sponsored by the G.E.C (E.S.B). It was a big deal to visit Dublin and it was a special day for me. The competition had a rule that it had to be brown soda bread and it had to be cooked in an electric cooker. Not every household would have had an electric cooker. We had the range at home so I practiced on the electric cooker in school. Ahead of the competition, I made bread every day in school and I was proud to represent my county."

MARY LYONS

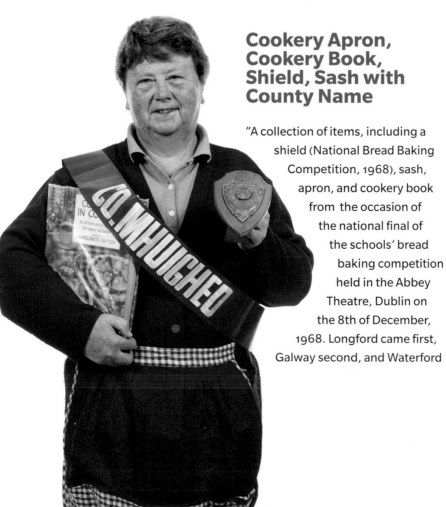

## Ironing Board

"This is an ironing board that my mother won in a baking competition. We were all very proud of it and still are. It is important to me because of the excitement we felt when she won it and also how useful it remains today given it's sturdiness. It was ultra modern at the time because you could slip the iron into the socket for it to heat. The prize also included a presser, which we no longer have. It's important for Ireland as it was one of the items used to promote electrification and improve the lives of women by reducing the time spent on domestic duties."

SIOBHÁN LONG

## Transistor Radio

"This is a transistor radio bought in Waterford in the mid 1950s. When electricity came to Mooncoin, this was the first appliance that my father William would have bought. It was in the house for a long time and was only replaced many years later when FM radio came out. The radio played in the kitchen all the time and was always at the centre of activity in the house. We used to listen to Dear Frankie, Gay Byrne, Sunday Miscellany with Ciarán Mac Mathúna, and, of course, all of the GAA games. There were sponsored shows on all the time too. That radio would have even broadcast the news of JFK's shooting and I'd say there wasn't a day over the course of forty years where this radio didn't play in our house."

RONAN WALSH

## 2lb Weighing Scales

"In the 1950s, this 2lb Brecknell weighing scales was supplied to Kathleen Shanaghy, The Market Cafe, 6 Coalmarket, Carlow by P.J. Kenny & Son, Enniscorthy. It sat on the counter of the shop in front of shelves lined with large jars of Cadburys and Oatfields sweets along with large glass-lidded tins of Jacobs and Bolands biscuits. The pan was shaped at each end for easy dispensing and weighing into paper bags. Behind the pan was a small circular spirit level that was centred using the four adjustable legs to ensure accuracy of the readings. The triangular screen facing the customer was to show them that the correct amount was dispensed while the one facing the shopkeeper also had a ready-reckoner scale that showed the price of the sale based on the price per pound of the item sold. If you had a business at the time, you had to comply with weight regulations so a Weights & Measures Inspector would regularly visit shops around Ireland to inspect the accuracy of the weights. When Kathleen retired in 1966, she sold the contents of the business but kept this treasured item for use as a kitchen scales in her home at Lacken House, Clogrennane, Carlow. Kathleen was my mother and this object was a big investment at the time for her starting a small shop. She was very attached to it and it has become a family heirloom."

NOEL SHANAGHY

## Cash Dispenser

"Prior to cash registers, retail outlets sent cash throughout the store using a dispenser that was attached to a pulley. When you took cash, you put it into the dispenser and pulled the pulley to send the dispenser up to the cash office on a wire. They would return the change via the dispenser. This one belonged to Floods Department Store in Terenure, a landmark at the time. I worked in the shop after school as a messenger boy and later on as an apprentice. The shop was a mixture of groceries, provisions, a chemist and a licensed premises next door. It was an old-school shop, no pre-packaged foods, and a great firm to work for. When I was there, there was a recession and earning a couple of bob was great for me. They provided a lot of employment around Terenure at the time. I remember we used to send up the odd dead mouse up to the office in these dispensers to frighten the girls. It was great fun. The store closed in 1968 coinciding with the emergence of supermarkets. The cash dispensers disappeared soon after."

PADDY HEFFERNAN

## Comptometor

"This is a calculator I used on a daily basis when I was employed by Associated Tailors in New Street, Dublin 8. I had to complete a course when I first started the job to teach me how to use it and it was the absolute height of technology at the time. When modern calculators were introduced, this comptometer was made redundant and it was going to be put in a skip, but I asked if I could keep it as a memento. I have very fond memories of that job and I've stayed in touch with many of the other women who worked there. There are not that many of us left but we still get together once a year to catch up and reminisce about happy times."

ANNE JOYCE

## An Irish-produced Swimsuit

"This swimsuit belonged to my mother and she loved it. It is from the late 50s, early 60s, and was made by Irish company Sunbeam in a factory in Blackpool on the Northside of Cork. I love the print, the butterflies, and the colours. I have it on display in my vintage clothes shop, Miss Daisy Blue, since we opened and it is the most asked-about item we have. Cork people are very surprised when they find out that it was made in Cork. We used to have a lot of clothes manufacturing in Ireland and objects like this are testaments to that story."

BREDA CASEY

## An Orchestral 'A' Machine

"This machine gave an orchestra an 'A' note to tune to. It belonged to the RTÉ National Symphony Orchestra. Today, orchestras use an oboe to tune to, but back in the day, RTÉ's Val Keogh, the orchestra manager, would head on to the stage of the St. Francis Xavier (SFX) Hall and turn on this machine. My uncle, Frank Young, who was the assistant manager of the orchestra, rescued it from a skip when they were leaving the SFX to the National Concert Hall. Frank was the sort of person who could see that it was a bit of history and he kept it. The machine still works and is incredibly accurate!"

GERARD KEENAN

## "World's Greatest Son" Trophy

"About 1957, my father made a trip from Limerick all along the west coast of Ireland right up to Donegal. We didn't know where he went but I guess my mum did. When he came back, he had this little souvenir from Bundoran for me, his youngest child. I've had it now for 60 years, moving from tops of televisions to sideboards to corners and it's a constant reminder to me that I had an extraordinary father. His name was Gerry Clancy and he was the last of the medieval guild of the Abbey Fishermen who were freshwater salmon fishermen in Limerick from medieval times to the 1930s. When this work was no longer possible following the construction of Ardnacrusha, my father became the caretaker for St. Mary's Hall in Limerick City. I always suspected that this change of career was difficult for him as he was an outdoors man at heart, but it was a choice he had to make in order to earn an income and support his family. Perhaps the trip he took along the coast in the late 50s was a nod to his former life as a fisherman and he regularly told us of the rugged beauty of Donegal. For me, this simple object is a symbol of the man my father was and it illustrates the love that I have for him."

KEVIN CLANCY

# BCG Information Leaflet

"This leaflet was used to spread information about the BCG vaccination and the dangers of tuberculosis. I am the little girl pictured in the leaflet and my uncle, Dr. John Cowell, was the medical director of the whole programme. It was 1952 and it would have been the very start of the BCG campaign. Tuberculosis would have been rampant up to that time. The vaccine was a "live vaccine" and it came in every Sunday from Sweden. I remember going to the airport with my uncle to collect it from the plane and he brought it to St. Ultan's where the BCG programme was based to get it refrigerated. He was very committed to the campaign. It was very successful and we are very proud of his role in eradicating tuberculosis in Ireland."

DEIRDRE GRATTAN

## Fixed Ankle Orthosis

"These are my fixed ankle orthosis (FAO) that make walking easier for me. They were made by the technicians at the Ottobock Group at Cappagh Hospital, Dublin under the guidance of Donna Fisher. Donna, a senior technician, has worked with me for many years now and created these FAOs six years ago. I am a polio survivor from the outbreak in Dublin in 1958. I was one year old at the time and I stayed in hospital subsequently for almost three years. We lived in Inchicore in Dublin, and because it was believed to be highly contagious, I wasn't allowed visitors or if I was, they visited me behind glass. I don't remember that time in my life; my memories of childhood are not of hospital, just memories of a happy childhood. I was blessed with my parents, as I'm sure they made exceptions for me but they treated me just like one of my sisters even though it must have been difficult. At the time, polio was viewed as a 'community disease', a public health issue, so I used to go to the corporation doctor and to a doctor in the hospital. With vaccinations, polio suddenly slipped from public consciousness. About 25 years ago, a group of survivors got together and created Polio Survivors Ireland, an advocate group. I have been using fixed ankle orthosis for about 15 years now and wear them every day."

JACKIE MINNOCK

## Circus Poster

"This is just one example from a huge array of circus posters and photos that I have in my possession from my late grandfather, John McCarthy. He grew up in Cappamore, Co. Limerick, and the travelling circuses used to set up in the field behind his home. He started collecting circus material from around 10 years of age and then later displayed them in his pub, McCarthy's Circus Bar. The collection starts from 1895 up until the 5th of February, 1966, when he died and I was born. All of the items I have in my possession were due to be thrown in a skip but thankfully, my father saved them. I am now the guardian of this collection."

TONY MCCARTHY

## Caul

"A caul is a thin membrane that can cover a newborn's head and face. Birth with a caul is rare, occurring in fewer than 1 in 80,000 births. The caul is harmless and is immediately removed by the physician or midwife upon delivery of the child. I was born with a caul but it was retained by the hospital. This caul belonged to my great grandfather, Terry Caulfield. Some believe those born with a caul are very lucky and immune from drowning for the rest of their lives, making them prized by sailors. Everybody who knows me would consider me lucky and luck has definitely played a huge role in my life. David Copperfield by Charles Dickens contains a scene where David is selling his caul at an auction. He describes the experience as very strange and the caul was bought by a sailor. I wouldn't sell this caul. It has been passed down through the generations and I will pass it down to the next."

TERRY O'REILLY

## A Catechism of Catholic Doctrine

"This is a small green book entitled *A Catechism of Catholic Doctrine*, first published in 1951. This edition was published in 1983 with a number of amendments. I was in national school in Curragh Camp, Kildare from 1956 to 1965 and would have used a catechism throughout this period. This book was a huge part of Irish school life for many years. As the book was focused on heaven and hell, our main aim as children was not to die with a sin or we would go straight to hell. Missing mass was considered a mortal sin! In many ways we lived with perpetual worry about sin and sinning. It seems so long ago now, but this document is a reminder of a certain time in Ireland when we believed so many things without a moment of doubt."

JOE MURRAY

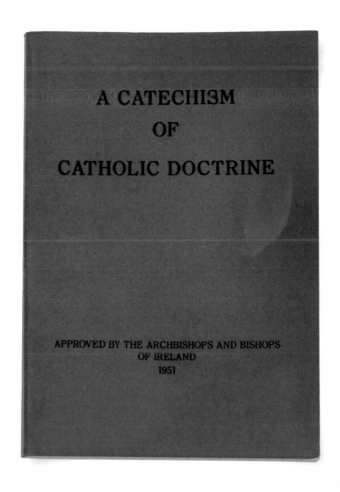

THE BIRTH OF OUR DIVINE LORD IN A STABLE AT BETHLEHEM

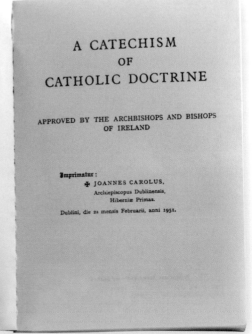

## A Selection of Objects from an Old Shed

"These are our Mamó's objects. She has held on to these objects for when we're older. There is a fire bellow from when she was a child, a Carinthia ship passenger list from when her father, a boxer, travelled to America for a match, and a Cow & Gate tin that was hers when she was a baby. We ask her all the time what life was like when she was our age. She tells us stories and shows us objects like these and the toys she has kept. She has a money box from when she was young, but it is empty."

MAYA LILY LAWLESS,
REUBEN LAWLESS AND
SOPHIA LAWLESS

## Scooter

"This object brings back some very fond memories of my childhood. It was a fifth birthday present and I rediscovered it in my parent's garden shed ten years ago. I had a huge circle of friends as a result of this scooter because everyone wanted to ride on it! It was the only one in the whole of Walkinstown. My grandchildren regularly play with this and my other toys that I've kept from my childhood. I've kept absolutely everything."

PATRICIA PENNY

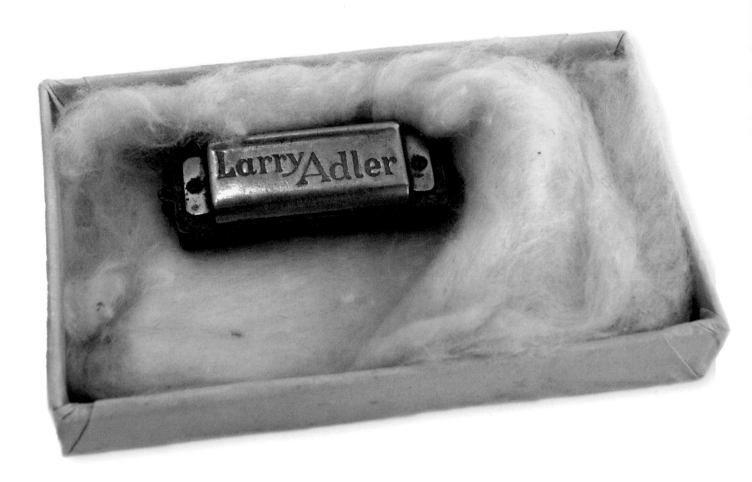

## Larry Adler's Mouth Organ

"Larry Adler was a famous American musician who played the mouth-organ (Adler preferred to call it this, not 'harmonica'). In August, 1950, Adler was to come to Dublin to perform in the Theatre Royal, but a controversy arose. John Charles McQuaid, the RC Archbishop of Dublin, wanted him banned, apparently because the U.S. House Committee on Un-American Activities (HUAC) had blacklisted Adler as a Communist. That concert didn't happen, but when Adler eventually did come to perform in Dublin, my father, who worked in the Theatre Royal, kept one of Adler's mouth-organs as a memento. My father was a firm believer in the separation of church and state, freedom of speech, and civil/ human rights, so he was appalled at the ban on performers. This became one of my father's prized possessions, mostly because of the controversy!"

DEIRDRE MOORE

## Theatre Royal "Last Night" Programme

"This is the final programme of the iconic Dublin variety theatre and cinema, the Theatre Royal, when it closed in 1962. It contains autographs of many Irish show business legends, including Cecil Sheridan, Babs de Monte, Alice Dalgarno, Bill Golding, Noel Purcell, and my father, Jim Bayle, a member of Jimmy Campbell's Theatre Royal Orchestra. For all of the Royal employees, the closing had a huge economic impact, including for my father. There were no redundancy payments and not many people got work in the theatre business after that. As a result, this object is iconic in our family's story."

CATHAL BAYLE

THEATRE ROYAL, DUBLIN
SATURDAY, 30th JUNE, 1962, at 8 p.m.
"ROYALE FINALE"

| | | |
|---|---|---|
| 1. | "PROLOGUE" | ... ... Jimmy Campbell and the Theatre Royal Orchestra. |
| 2. | "SHOW BUSINESS" | ... Frankie Blowers, Peggy Dell, Royalettes, Jimmy Campbell Singers. |
| 3. | "TREBLE TROUBLE" | ... Cecil Sheridan, Mickser Reid, John Molloy, Derry O'Donovan. |
| 4. | "MUSICAL COCKTAIL" | ... Jimmy Campbell Singers. |
| 5. | "A ROYAL OCCASION" | ... Cecil Sheridan and John Molloy. |
| 6. | ENSEMBLE | ... ... Alice Dalgarno, Babs de Monte, Royalettes, Cora Cadwell Dancers and the Jimmy Campbell Singers. |

INTERVAL:
"ROYAL CABARET"
OUR GUESTS :

Frankie Blowers
Paddy Crosbie
Val Fitzpatrick
Frank Howard
Jimmy O'Dea
Milo O'Shea

Edmund Browne
Danny Cummins
Pauline Forbes
Josef Locke
Harry O'Donovan

Jack Cruise
Ursula Doyle
Vernon Hayden
Sean Mooney
Noel Purcell

Mickser Reid      Cecil Sheridan
Choreography and Design : Alice Dalgarno and Babs De Monte
The Jimmy Campbell Singers :
Kay Condron Denis Claxton Claire Kelleher Bill Golding Dolores Murphy
The Royalettes
JIMMY CAMPBELL and the THEATRE ROYAL ORCHESTRA
TOMMY DANDO

**Little Arrows - The Dixies**
Save The Last Dance For Me · Dream Lover · Ebony Eyes
Don't Let The Stars Get In Your Eyes · and others

## *Little Arrows:* The Dixies

"This L.P. is a reminder of the great showband boom of the 1960s and early 1970s. It brings back memories of growing up in North Cork at that time and of going to dance halls like The Majestic in Mallow, The Mayflower in Mitchelstown, and The Top Hat in Fermoy. It was a more innocent time. There was no alcohol allowed, and girls stood on one side and boys on the other (oh, that dreaded walk across the floor hoping some pretty girl wouldn't turn you down!). The show bands played cover versions of current pop songs, like from this Dixies' LP. Homegrown stars like Brendan Bowyer, Dickie Rock, and Cork's own The Dixies were big attractions. These dances were the main social outlet for young people in rural Ireland at this time and drew crowds from a radius of thirty or more miles. Young Ireland was on the move and the days of dancing at the crossroads were over!"

DENIS CRONIN

## Philips Tape Recorder

"I bought this tape recorder for myself in 1959 for entertainment in Clancy's shop in Glenfarne, Co. Leitrim. I did a lot of recording with it at concerts and variety shows in Glenfarne's famous Ballroom of Romance. It used to have a handheld microphone and I was able to record six musicians at a time in the hall. I used it for twenty or thirty years and I recorded many of the bands from the showband days on it, such as Big Tom, Clipper Carlton, Melody Aces, and Dave Glover. Unfortunately, my recordings were damaged but I am now collecting and archiving the showband era, having created a small museum in the Ballroom of Romance, which includes this object."

GERRY FINNERAN

## Mantilla

"This is my mantilla headscarf that I wore to church when I was young. The tradition at the time was that all women had to cover their heads going to mass. When I wore it, I thought I was very grown up. It was a very beautiful object and I thought I was very mature, just like the older ladies. I remember my aunt in particular, Noreen Ennis, having a nice mantilla with some very fine lace work. In a way, the mantilla was a way to express yourself in that there were degrees of sophistication in the headscarves and mantillas that women wore. I didn't really understand why I was wearing it and, much like everyone else, I wouldn't have understood what was said during the mass as it was in Latin, but we just accepted it for what it was. After the Second Vatican Council (Pope John XXIII), young women no longer had to cover their heads anymore. Priests could say mass in the vernacular as well, and the laity could be more involved. Despite being relegated to the bottom of the drawer, I've kept my mantilla for over 50 years."

MARY ENNIS

## Jacob's Tins

"These vintage storage tins belonged to my grandmother, Mary Linehan, and were always in the house as far as I can remember. She used to hide the cream crackers in them away from the children and grandchildren, but they were always found eventually. Jacob's Cream Crackers have been a family favourite over the generations from my grandmother to my own son who is now six. When my grandfather passed away a few years ago, we were clearing out the house and these were found in the shed with a few rusty nails in them. I cleaned them up and brought them into my kitchen where they have been on display ever since. They are a really simple but special part of my family history and I don't think I will ever do away with them."

SADHBH COSTIGAN

## Clancy Brothers Aran Sweater

"In 1961, the Clancy Brothers were trying to break America. They were touring and struggling to survive a cold winter. Hearing how cold it was, the mother of the Clancy Brothers sent sweaters over to the four singers and when the group's manager saw them wearing the sweaters, he said, "That's what we need! Something distinctly Irish." The sweaters became their trademark as they started to become successful, especially following their appearance on the Ed Sullivan Show wearing Aran Sweaters. In the early summer of 1963, my husband, Paddy Clancy, and I were travelling to Co. Mayo to visit my parents. We stopped off in Spiddal, Co. Galway, to visit the famous shop of Standuns and look at the stock of Irish clothing, and maybe find a new sweater or two for the exciting new life as folk singers these fellows were recently enjoying in America. Paddy was surprised at the warm exuberant welcome extended to him. It was very exciting for the owner to have one of this new group in the flesh wandering around his shop floor because they had not yet performed in Ireland. We looked at the luscious merchandise. Paddy picked out a beautifully knitted polo neck jumper made with genuine Aran wool. It was his favourite sweater. He had many sweaters over the years, but this one travelled many thousands of miles with him. He was tall and slim and the lines and patterning of the delicate knitting suited his trim frame. It was only very delicately hand washed by me using water. I didn't like putting it into soapy water, so it's still feels like wool. There's a red marker stain on the inside of the collar that reminded Paddy which is the front and which is the back of the jumper as he was running on to the stage."

MARY CLANCY

## A Catholic Handbook

"This little booklet measuring 9cm x 11,5cm, which cost sixpence highlights a very different Ireland. Published in 1954, the handbook was drawn up because "economic difficulties especially the scarcity of work in counties like Mayo, Kerry and Galway have caused boys and girls to leave homes in Ireland and seek a living in the land across the water." When I took up my first teaching post in Roscommon in 1974, it was part of the library in the school. I was given the responsibility to sort out the school library and when I found this document, I decided to keep it because it speaks volumes about Ireland at a certain period in time. You wouldn't know whether to laugh or cry reading it but when I first read it, I recognised its historical value. In many ways, it was sad that it was a reference book in a school library where many students would have emigrated from. It gives insight into the loneliness, isolation, and fear of emigration in the 1950s. On arrival in England, the book advises that one of the first things you should do is look up the local parish priest."

EILEEN FAHEY

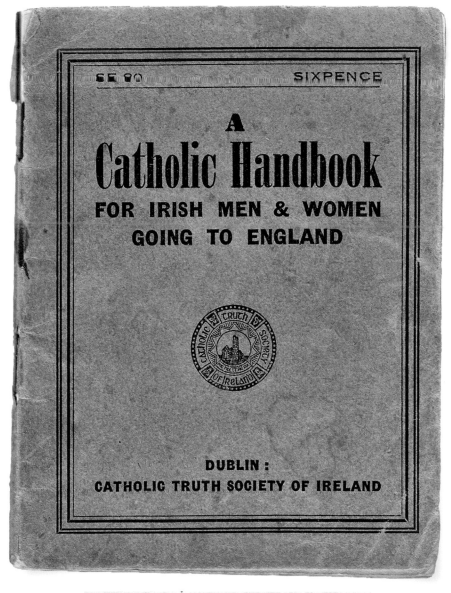

A
**Catholic Handbook**
FOR IRISH MEN & WOMEN
GOING TO ENGLAND

SIXPENCE

DUBLIN :
CATHOLIC TRUTH SOCIETY OF IRELAND

Church." On arrival at your destination, do two things as soon as possible—(1) go to see the friend whose address you have and talk things over with him (or her) and (2) leave at the Parish Priest's house a slip of paper giving your name, age and address and stating that, having come from Ireland, you are staying in the parish at least for a few weeks. If you have not got a job awaiting you, go to the Labour Exchange and get a temporary one so that you can start work at once. Open a Post Office Savings Bank Book and put in it at least five to ten shillings a week, over and above whatever money you send home to your family. This money will be a great help later on. Make sure of beginning well with God's blessing by going to Confession on your very first Saturday in England and Communion the following day; never say "Oh, I'll leave it till next week." The next task is to find permanent lodgings and a job which you will like and keep. Your temporary lodgings and your first job may suit. But think over the question carefully for a few weeks and talk about

11

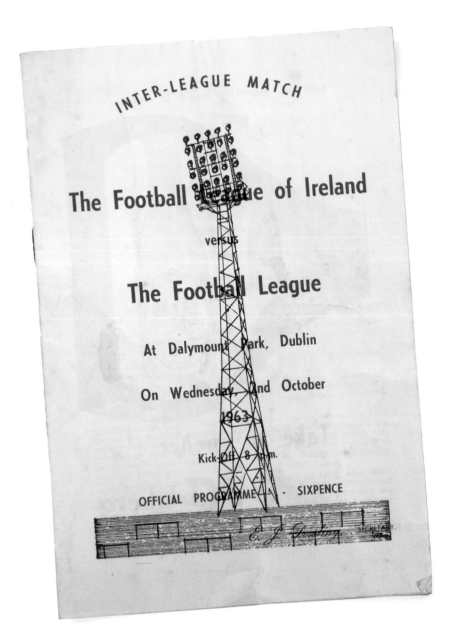

## 1963 League of Ireland XI v England FA XI Football Programme

"This football match programme from October 1963, celebrates a famous night in Irish football when the Football League of Ireland beat the English Football League 2-1 at Dalymount Park, Dublin, before a crowd of over 25,000 excited fans. The *Irish Independent* headline the following day read 'Carve Their Names In Pride' (a play on the title of the big movie in town at the time), honouring part-timers and one amateur who beat the professionals of the football league, a side including eventual World Cup winners Jimmy Armfield, Bobby Moore, and manager, Alf Ramsey. Ronnie Whelan Senior, a member of the League of Ireland team, scored the winning goal that night, and the story goes that he missed the team training session because he was working the night shift that week, and he only joined his team mates on the day of the game after his supervisor gave him the time off to play at Dalymount. Many of the team were part-timers and my uncle, Willie Browne from Longford, was the only full amateur member of the team that evening. For me, this object is a reminder of the glory days of League of Ireland football."

RICHARD BROWNE

## Football Boots

"These are my old muddied football boots from when I played for Limerick FC in 1960. In that year, we won the league and subsequently played Young Boys Berne in Europe. I have the programme for that match. I remember that when we went over to Switzerland, Young Boys had a whole cage full of footballs while we had only four with us! Our manager told us to not to kick any balls into the crowd as we had so few. Back in those days, boots had a really hard layer underneath and the studs were nailed through. Sometimes the studs would come through and your feet would be all bloodied."

WILLIAM CLINTON

## Indenture Cert from the Glin Industrial School

"This document is just one item from a series of documents I have in my possession from Glin Industrial School. The documents are a complete record of boys that attended an industrial school in Co. Limerick. This specific document illustrates that when the children were finished in the industrial school, they had to pay the wages from their first three years at work back to the manager of the school and all they received was food, lodgings, and clothing. In my opinion, it shows that the school exploited these boys and is in essence a slave document. I myself was brought up in this industrial school. In 1966, when I turned 16, the school was closed down and I was kept on to work on the farm of the property. I remained there, employed by the Christian Brothers for seven years until 1973 when the property was entirely vacated by the last few Brothers. There were a very large number of records, letters, and other documents in the school's office and the superior asked me to put a number of the ledgers into the boot of his car. He then ordered me to get rid of all of the other documents. Knowing that some documents related to myself might be included in these records, I kept a number of boxes. These boxes remained in the attic of my house in Limerick for over forty years until five years ago when a damaged roof caused me to rediscover them. When looking through the documents, I did indeed discover items related to myself, including a letter that my aunt had sent me as a child that had been confiscated and never reached me. It is very important to me that these records are maintained and that people know what happened in these institutions."

THOMAS WALL

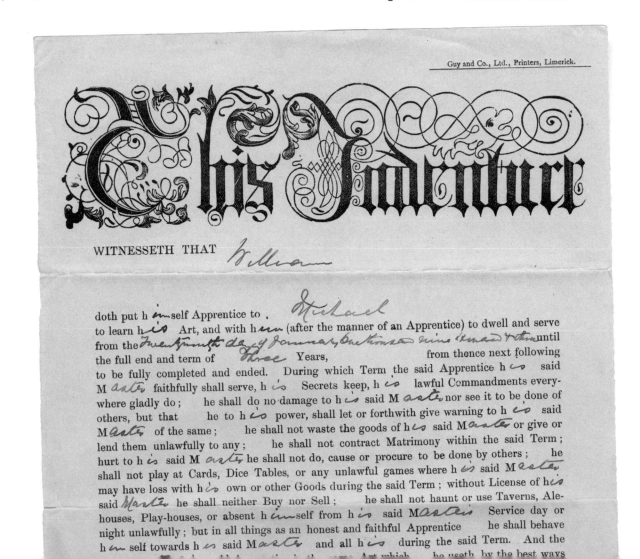

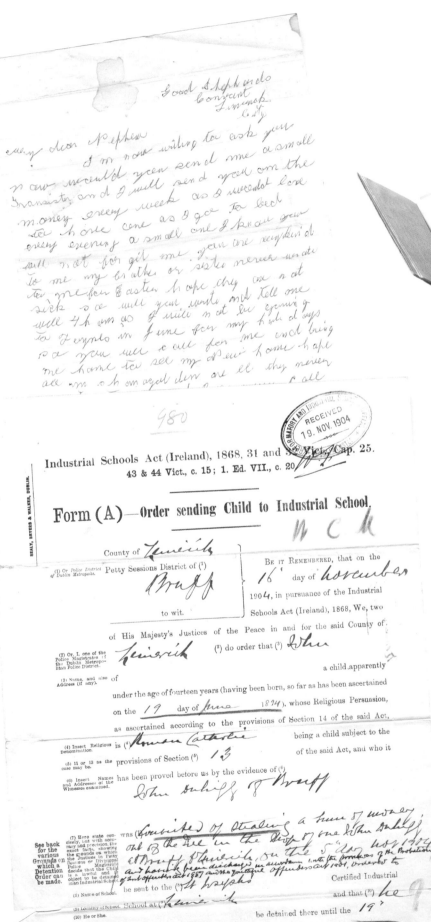

## All in the Cooking

"I used this cookbook in Athlone Tech in the early 1960s. It was the official school cooking textbook sponsored by the Dublin Vocational Education Committee. Every Friday in school was for cookery class and I remember cooking stuffed lamb liver with rasher wrapped around it, sponge cakes, rice puddings, etc. I remember our teacher said when we finished cooking, 'A place for everything and everything in its place.' It's a great little book and explains things so well. I still use it and these days my children are now using it too."

ROSE KELLY

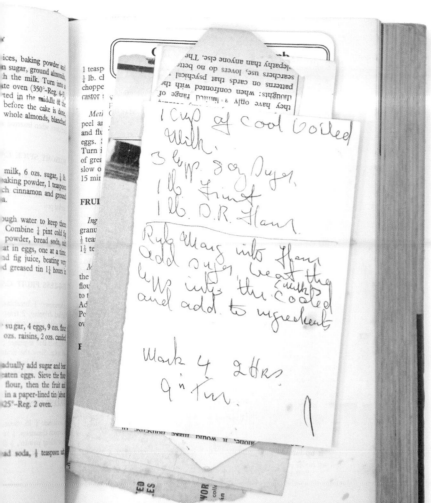

## Maura Laverty's
### *Full and Plenty*

"This textbook was used in my home economics class at school and by my mother for years afterwards at home. It was a staple in many Irish kitchens, and this one includes the addition of some of my mother's own recipes. When I left home and moved away to Dublin, my mother held on to it and it did not come back into my possession until she passed away many years later."

MARY MORRISSEY

## Array of Items from a Pharmacy

"My father was a pharmacist and he bought a shop in Thurles in 1962 that was originally established as Pharmacy Way in 1889. The shop was in its original state and within it, he found these objects among many others. My father, Donal P. Sammon, never threw anything out and kept all the old artefacts he found. The objects include old poison bottles, powders, and a cut-throat razor. My father continued the shop as a pharmacy from 1962 to 2004. I took over from him then and the pharmacy is still going strong. As a pharmacist, I find these objects really interesting. Back then, a pharmacist had to mix medicine in the shop. Opium, cocaine, arsenic, and morphine were regularly used. Thankfully, we don't have to do that today!"

CARMEL SAMMON

## Delivery Box from Curtin's Shop

"This is a box from my grandmother's shop on Talbot Street, Dublin 1. Molly Curtin came to Dublin from rural east Clare in 1918. Initially, she worked in her older sister's shop and then she set up on her own in 1926. Molly chose Talbot Street as it was convenient to Connolly Station, making it accessible 'to women from the country'. Molly ran the shop there for nearly 50 years selling 'mantles and gowns' (wedding dresses were a specialty) all handmade by a team of seamstresses in a workshop to the rear. She finally retired when she was in her mid 70s. About 10 years ago, my brother spotted this box being used in a jewellery store in Dublin as part of their window display. He explained his interest in it and the shop owner let him take it away. It sits on a shelf in my parents' home now. I enjoy the connection it provides with our family history and I'm always amused that clothes I buy now, 80 years later, are quite often delivered by a courier to my doorstep packaged in a brown cardboard box."

NESSA WALSH

## The Boru Cape by Jimmy Hourihan

"My mother, Clare McKervey, was given a present of this gorgeous Boru label cape by her sister Margaret as a thank you for minding her four children for a week. It was made by Irish manufacturer Jimmy Hourihan, a brand still involved in producing capes. The Boru label is over fifty years old. This cape is from an early collection. My mum loved it and wore it for years. I wear it now. As a child, the colours made me think of falling leaves, and when she took the cape out of her wardrobe, it meant that summer was over and autumn had begun."

HENRIETTA MCKERVEY

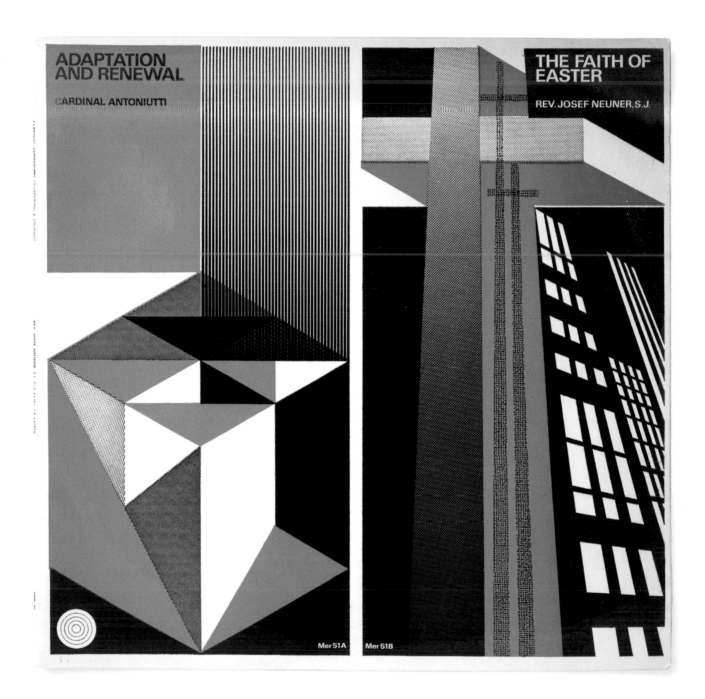

## Cor Klassen-Designed, Catholic Church, Post-Vatican II Album for Mercier Press

"This album from 1969 is one of a set of religious albums issued by Mercier Press in Cork. It features cover art by Cor Klaasen, which is the reason I've chosen this as a worthy object. Klassen was from Holland originally but became an Irish citizen in 1962. He designed covers for multiple Irish books and records during the 1960s and 1970s. Many of the books were school books and are likely to resonate with thousands of school goers from that period. His striking covers made school days more colourful and opening those dreaded books a little more interesting. This album cover forms part of a vintage Irish pop culture and lifestyle archive I created called Brand New Retro."

BRIAN MCMAHON

## Picture of Pope John 23<sup>rd</sup>, JFK and Pope Paul 6<sup>th</sup>

"I'm not sure whether this is a religious object, a political object, or a reflection of emigration in Ireland. It used to hang in my grandmother's house. She was born in America but her family returned to Ireland shortly after. One of her relatives brought this object back from America around 1962. Images of popes and images of John F. Kennedy hung on almost every wall in Ireland but this picture is unusual in that three big icons from the time are all pictured together in one frame surrounded by some glitter. I think it reflects what the ordinary people of Ireland felt was important at the time and also JFK's standing in Irish society as being equal to a pope."

MARY MCGING

## JFK Viewmaster

"This is a unique collection of photos from the time of JFK's visit to Ireland and has been in our family since the 1960s. The Viewmaster gives an impression of 3D and this one illustrates various parts of JFK's visit when he came to Ireland in 1963. The item is still in its original box and in perfect condition. All we had in Ireland in those days was black and white TV so this object that presented colour 3D images was truly amazing at the time. JFK was hugely popular and, like most Irish people, we were very excited when he came to visit Ireland. Sadly, he was shot and killed only five months later. I was eight at the time of his death and remember I was playing in the back garden when my father came out and told us he had died. In the years that have followed, we always understood the value of this object and how it tells a very important part of the Irish story. This is why it still remains in our family."

GERALDINE CORCORAN

## US Army Duffel Bag

"The fate of many early Irish emigrants was to be drafted into the US Army. On emigrating from a small farm in Mullaghmore, Co. Sligo in 1961, I was drafted into the army a mere ten months after arriving in New York. This was during the period of US involvement in Vietnam. Everything I owned was packed into this canvas bag and carried around for the two years of full-time service, first in Fort Dix, New Jersey, then Fort Belvoir, Virginia, and then to Evreux Fauville airbase in France. The mission there was 'supply by sky' where supplies were air dropped into Vietnam, Cambodia, and Laos. Four years in the reserves followed full-time service when I was given an honourable discharge into civilian life again. I met many Irish who also served during that time."

JOE MCGOWAN

## Cosaint Shibhialta
### *Bás Beatha*

"This is a manual issued to all Irish households to prepare people for the prospect of nuclear war. The book came with a pre-punched hole in the top left corner with a ribbon so it could be displayed prominently in the household and be easily accessible. It contains information about the national alert strategy that would inform people and encourages them to help each other survive a nuclear fallout. It also contains advice on first aid, managing livestock, and protecting against radiation, with some nuggets including covering your potato crops with soil, filling the bath with water, and putting wardrobes filled with top soil against the windows of your house. It was produced around the time of the Cuban Missile Crisis and I received it via my in-laws. The only page that shows any use is the chapter on first aid."

DAVID MCKENNA

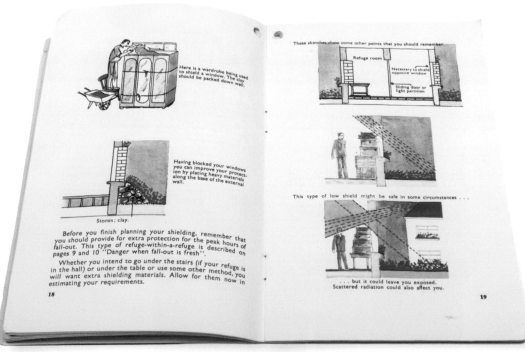

## Soundings

"*Soundings* was the poetry anthology for the Leaving Certificate curriculum and it was the basis for the poetry course from 1969 for thirty years. It was complied by Augustine Martin of University College Dublin and is remarkable for its ambition and the high degree of critical engagement it demands from Leaving Cert students. The books themselves became totems of nostalgia and trophies of study, and can often be found with doodles, marginal notes, and highlights that represent an individual student's learning. We had to learn chunks of Milton's Lycidas off by heart. It is a great gift to have that, and I remember reciting 'But oh! The heavy change now thou art gone, Now thou art gone and never must return... '. When George Harrison died, I pinned it up on the notice board at work - 'Thee [Beatle], thee the woods and desert caves, With the wild thyme and gadding vine o'ergrown, And all their echoes mourn.' I think it's what Milton would have wanted."

FINTAN O'HIGGINS

## JFK Brooch

"This is my JFK brooch from when I was a young girl. I loved the Kennedys and I used to have a scrapbook where I collected every photo of the Kennedys I could find. I got this brooch made in a jewellers in Cork using a coin that had JFK's face on it. I had it made a few years after JFK's death and the Kennedys were still big news. The family were like a fairytale, a Camelot story, and I wore this brooch on my coat all the time. When you're young, you're so impressionable and I am still interested in the Kennedys."

MARGARET HACKETT

MAKING AND USING
**IRISH LINEN**

THE IRISH LINEN GUILD

## Lace & Linen Collection

"My Father worked in the Linen Industry and was a tenter by trade, fixing the looms. He learned his trade with Richardsons Mill in a Quaker village in Bessbrook and following this he also worked for Robinsons and Cleavers in their factory in Banbridge. These items are of significance to all the people associated with the linen industry In Ireland."

CAROLINE FEEHAN

## Collection of Irish Linen

"This is a collection of Irish linen from the 1950s to the 1980s. When I moved into my husband's house in the 90s, I discovered lots of linen hidden away in the attic. They were most likely collected by his mother or received as gifts over the years. I was really taken by them, especially the range of patterns and the stories they tell. The designs include nature, animals, fruits, flowers, farming scenes, and sometimes advertising. I never met my husband's mother as she had died about six months before we started dating, so these objects are a nice connection between me and her."

SHARON O'MAHONY

## Irish Union of Woodworkers Rules Booklet

"We had a huge tradition of furniture manufacturing in Ireland, especially in Navan, which was considered the 'Home of Furniture'. Sadly, from the 70s right through to 2000, the industry saw a huge decline. My father, John Vesey, held this book (amongst others) proudly as a reminder of that era. His passion was wood and he loved to pass on his craft. He was there from the beginning of the industry in Navan and witnessed its rise and fall. He was a master craftsman, wood turner, cabinet maker, and part-time teacher and he, along with local legends including frame makers, upholsterers, polishers and carvers formed the Irish Union of woodworkers in the Navan area, mainly to unite different craftsmen in the areas and to create a better product. Knowledge was key as they had to compete with the larger companies in the UK market, which they did with great success, managing to put Navan on the world map."

BRIANÁN VESEY

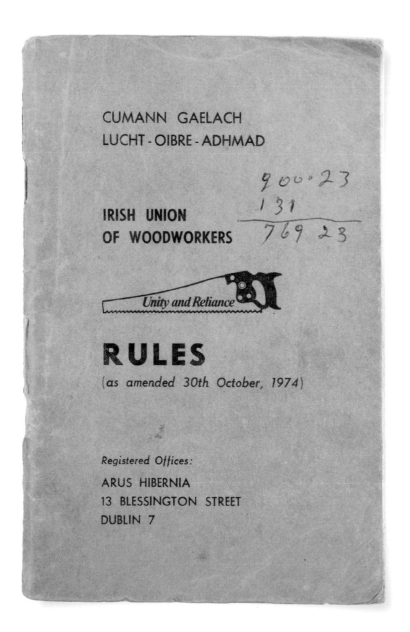

## Crannac
## Model C Chair

"I grew up with a three-piece suite that I considered dated and unfashionable. My mother had a sentimental attachment to the suite as it had belonged to her mother and my grandmother, Blath Ní Aogain. Blath was a graduate of NCAD in the late 1950s and loved design. It is only in more recent years that I appreciate the place this furniture, had not just in my mother's heart but in the history of Irish contemporary furniture production. The suite was from the Navan based company, Crannac, a range called the Model C. Crannac furniture was high in quality and contemporary in design, and was exported worldwide. The design has a clean-lined Scandinavian influence. The frames are made from Afrormosia timber from Ghana and finished with an oil that preserved the natural features of the wood. The refurbished suite has moved with us, fitting seamlessly into our new contemporary home. Good design does not date and the suite still contributes to the functionality and quality of our everyday lives. My grandmother passed away before I was born, but her love of life, art, and good design lives on and is remembered daily through our Crannac suite."

ALEX LLOYD

## Dick Tracy Cap Gun

"This Dick Tracy cap gun has been in my possession since I was a young boy and it brings back great memories. These guns and Dick Tracy generally were very popular with little boys in the 6os. Everyone wanted to be a detective, including myself, and I was a top dog with this gun. In those days, comics were popular and we used to swap them for toys and for other comics. Old comics were called 'stailers' and you used to swap three 'stailers' for a new comic. The comics were either DC or Dell. Not only were there plenty of Dick Tracys on the streets of Ballyfermot, but there were cowboys and there were Indians, all of us running around playing cap guns, marbles and skipping, having the time of our lives. Life for a child back then was all outside; our parents had to drag us in at night time. This cap gun brings back the fantastic memories of my childhood. It still works, but unfortunately I can't find caps for it."

MICHAEL BANEHAM

## *Ryan's Daughter*
## Guinness Bottle

"David Lean was such a perfectionist that when he was making *Ryan's Daughter*, he got Guinness to produce a special Guinness label to put on the bottles on the shelves of T. Ryan's pub in Kirrary (The Ryan's Daughter Village). When the film was completed, the five landowners at Slea Head couldn't agree on keeping the film set intact, which would have been one of the country's greatest tourist attractions. The entire village of Kirrary was cleared by the production company and the land returned to nature. I understand all the bottles were also destroyed, but for a handful and this is one of the remaining ones with the label still on the bottle."

DEREK COBBE

## Collection of Wicker Items

"My mother, Nancy Casey, was a prominent member of the ICA (Irish Countrywoman's Association) in Kilbeacanty, Co. Galway, and she was also a very creative woman. The ICA would have been the only social outing for local people at the time as we lived in a very rural area in the foothills of the Slieve Aughty Mountains. There were up to 60 members back then in the 1970s. Activities at the meetings included knitting, crochet, sewing, and many other crafts, but my mother was particularly talented at wicker work. When I was old enough, I joined the ICA too and went along with my mother. I also loved creating items from wicker. The objects in this photo were all made by myself and my mother and they include a tray, a baby basket, a shopping bag, and a vase holder. Also included in the photo is another piece (dark brown in colour), which is a muzzle for a calf that was made by my grandmother long before I became involved with the ICA. These objects are a symbol of the huge role that the ICA played

in the social history of rural Irish women and are also a wonderful connection between me, my mother, and my grandmother."

ANNA CASEY-DONOHUE

## Poster for 'Cultural Relations Committee of Ireland' Designed by Patrick Scott

"I am a designer and a collector of Irish ephemera. I was at an auction in 2012 and bought this poster. It was misattributed in the catalogue, and I bought it speculatively. Fortunately, a friend identified it as being designed by well-known Irish artist, Patrick Scott. In 2012, the artist was still alive and I knew him via a friend (I had done some work for him in the late 1970s). I mentioned it to the mutual friend and it transpired that Scott himself did not have a copy of this poster. Before he died in 2014, he was kind enough to give me the colour separations that he originally made to produce this poster in the late 50s. It was created for the Cultural Relations Committee of Ireland and printed by Hely's in Dublin. The poster's title is "Pagan and Early Christian Ireland," which I find quite revealing of attitudes in Ireland at the time; definitions such as Neolithic, Bronze Age, or Iron Age were all gathered under the one heading: 'Pagan'! It seems a very Church-centric view, with historic sites classified as either being Christian or non-Christian. I loaned the poster to the Irish Museum of Modern Art for a retrospective exhibition of Patrick Scott's work in 2014. Very few of these posters survive, as the paper quality wasn't good."

WENDY WILLIAMS

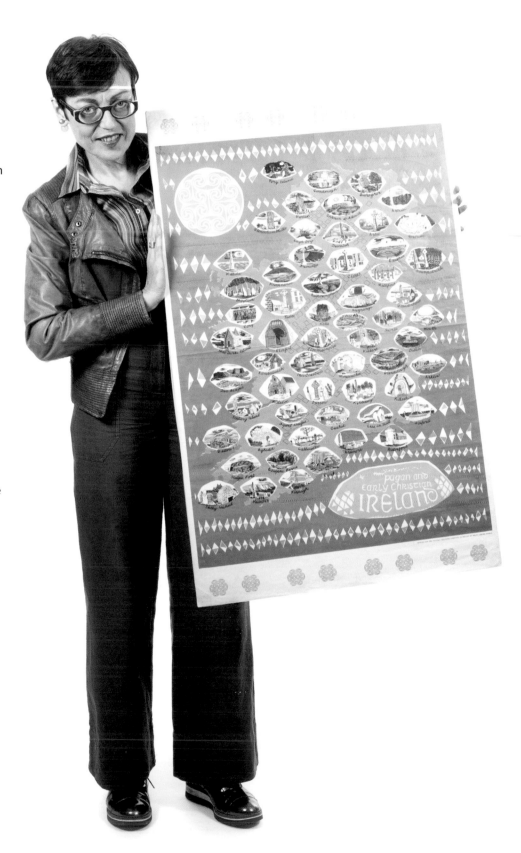

## Plastic Bullet

"After returning from Australia in 1976, I worked as a substitute teacher in Holy Cross Boys School in the Ardoyne area of Belfast. This area experienced more than its fair share of the devastation caused by what is euphemistically called the 'Troubles'. Army raids and shootings were daily occurrences and no one suffered the fallout more than the children. Getting to school meant negotiating army roadblocks and picking up the debris of the latest riot. When an eight year old I was teaching presented me with this plastic bullet, I didn't know what it was but he was quick to explain, "It's a plastic bullet, Miss. The Brits shot my mate with this one. You can have it. I can get plenty more". The plastic bullet was introduced to Northern Ireland in 1973 to replace the rubber bullet, which had been used for 'crowd control' since 1970. The plastic bullet was thought to be less lethal than the rubber bullet, which was said to have been capable of ricocheting and causing widespread damage in a crowd. For years, families have called for an investigation into the lethal use of plastic bullets, but according to the Pat Finucane Centre, the files will remain closed until 2047."

PATRICIA SHEARER

## Clothes Made from a H-Block Blanket

"These are items of clothing made from Long Kesh protest blankets as part of an art project to highlight the anniversary of the beginning of the blanket protest in 1976. I am an ex-prisoner who was involved in the blanket protests and I was also involved in the hunger strike in which Bobby Sands died. I feel that by adapting the blanket into elegant garments, we have symbolically illustrated how our communities have moved on from our troubled past without forgetting what happened during those difficult times."

LAURENCE MCKEOWN

## Coins with Loyalist Markings

"These are Irish coins that were stamped with loyalist emblems during the Troubles and sent back into circulation. They were acquired by my late father and passed on to me. My father was very passionate about Irish military history and collected many items over the years. He would have deemed these as a significant part of the Irish story. This series of coins, including animal imagery, are quite iconic and this defacement therefore sends a very powerful message. For me, they are a poignant reminder of a very dark part of our history."

PHILIPPE O'SULLIVAN

## Long Kesh Bags

"These bags were made when I was in Long Kesh prison in 1974/1975 when jailed as part of the armed struggle. This was before the Hunger Strike; we had political status at the time. We received letters from support groups and we made these objects for those support groups to raffle and raise money. We also made them for family. They are pure leather and have never been used, just kept for posterity."

PATRICK MCMENAMIN

## Adult Magazines

"These are some early editions of Irish men's magazines, *Man Alive* and *Executive*. *Man Alive* first hit the top shelves in Irish newsagents back in 1974 and described itself as 'Ireland's first magazine for Men'. Printed and published in Ireland and styled on the popular American magazine *Playboy*, it featured short stories, interviews, fashion, cars, art, and cartoons mostly by Irish writers and artists. The magazines also featured photographic essays; in other words, colour spreads of semi-nude women."

SINEAD KENNY

## "National" Brand Television

"I call this object "The Box." The model number is TR-475G National transistor. The TV is transistorised and is without valves, which determines that the age of the object is post-1960. It is a portable device with a top handle. The top section flips open to reveal a compact TV screen with adjustable controls. There is a 4.5 inch screen. It is still operational, but you'd have to connect a Saorview box! I am an avid antique collector and have collected all sorts of things for the past 50 years. My interest in collecting started out with TVs when my mother's TV broke and I decided to repair it myself."

MICHAEL FOY

## Esso All-Ireland Amateur Drama Fest Trophies

"These trophies were won in what was formally known as the Esso All Ireland Drama Festival. The Amateur Drama Movement (ADM) and the festival was created as a social activity for young people and communities to be involved in during Lent, when dancing was forbidden. Over our 40 years of treading the boards, the Amateur Drama Movement (ADM) offered members the opportunity to travel, to make friendships with people all across Ireland and, in some ways, it was better than a university degree. The Drama Festival however was not just about winning trophies. It provided the people and communities involved with a structured social outlet when there was high emigration, high unemployment, and the disadvantages of low incomes. It offered entertainment and education to players and audiences alike. In a time of very few outlets, the amateur productions gave a chance of achievement, the chance of escape from the humdrum, and added a bit of spice to life. The ADM was also a doorway for many amateurs to turn professional. The ADM and ensuing festivals have offered thousands of participants the chance to socialise, to learn, and the space in which to do it. In our case, which is not unique to us, it has led to a love of theatre and the arts over a fifty year period and we are still going strong!"

GERRY & PATRICIA KING

## DeLorean Factory Plans

"I purchased these plans in 1999 in Mother Redcaps market for three pounds. The plans show the layout of the factory where the famous DeLorean car from 'Back to the Future' was made. I was browsing the market and looking at an old iron fireplace when I pulled out the grate, the plans were crumpled up in a ball inside (along with a secondary copy, which were not in quite as good condition). The cars were made in the factory for four years, but sales quickly dropped and John DeLorean went bankrupt. In 1982 he was arrested for drug trafficking charges (but was never charged) and the factory was shut down."

MICHAEL O'REILLY

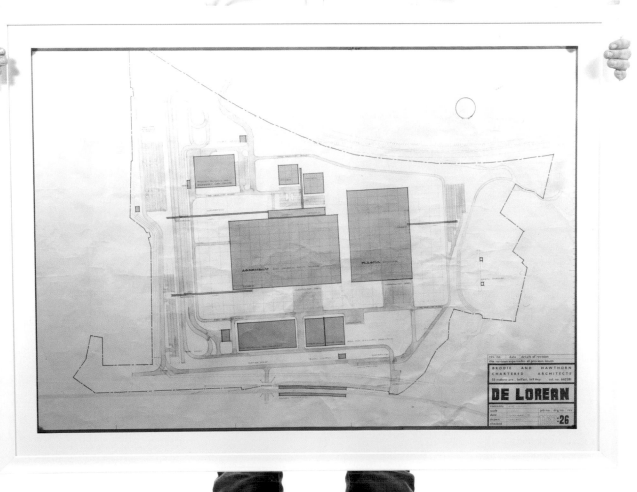

## Crolly Doll in a Silver Cross Pram

"This is my Crolly Dolly in a doll-size Silver Cross pram. I have a whole collection of dolls from my childhood, but this one is my favourite. I love her. I received the dolly from Father Christmas when I was five and I have held on to it ever since. The Crolly Dolly was made in Donegal and my mother made her new clothes regularly. I kept everything from my childhood as they are my memories from a fabulous time in my life. Once a year, I take all my dollies out and wash their hair with my two girls. That is the only day of the year that my girls are allowed to play with them."

CAROLINE MCGRATH

## An Enamel on Copper Bowl

"This is a bowl designed and produced by well-known smith, Pádraig Ó Mathúna, who is primarily known for his work with silver. This bowl is one of his rare works in copper. It's hand-beaten and has a layer of brown enamel on top. It's important to me because of the craft, the art, and the skill involved in making it."

CLAIRE STACK

## Dance Club Membership Card from 1976

"This is my late sister, Mary Naughton's, membership card to the Zhivago Club, a supper night club and discotheque in Dublin. There were dance halls and then there was the Zhivago Club. They had DJs playing the latest hits and it was a totally different venue. It was trendy and hip. I used to borrow my sister's card to get in. As the radio ad used to say, 'Love stories begin at the Zhivago', and for me a love story did begin there when I met my future husband on the dance floor in 1972."

CLAIRE O'BRIEN

## 1978 Munster v All Blacks Match Programme

"This is a match programme from the famous Munster vs. All Blacks game in 1978 when Munster won 12-0. I'm a huge rugby fan and I was lucky enough to be a steward at the game, positioned at the very front of the stand on the halfway line. I was working in a small bank at the time and it was only at the very last minute on the morning of the match that my boss actually gave me permission to attend. This was one of the greatest All Blacks teams ever and Munster's victory over them is regarded as one of the most famous moments in Ireland's rugby history."

DEREK BROWNE

## Radio Luxembourg 208 T-Shirt

"I remember my 'good old days' in boarding school. We listened regularly to Radio Luxembourg surreptitiously in the dormitory with a radio hidden under the blankets. I remember the 'power play' when the station selected a particular record to be played hourly for a week. A major power play that I recall from those days was 'Make me an Island" by Joe Dolan. Later, I heard the announcement of the death of Elvis Presley on Radio Luxembourg. The announcement stays in my memory to this day. First, the station said, 'We have a major news story on the next hour.' The next bulletin went something like, 'The King is dead' and continued, 'But we are a commercial station so we will continue as normal, and they went on to cover the remaining news. However, on the following bulletin, they started, 'The King is dead. Indeed, there is no other news. The directors have decided that there will be no more advertising tonight'. Those were the days and this t-shirt reminds me of that time!"

GEOFFREY MCMASTER

## Bottle of Babycham

"This is a bottle of Babycham saved from my first Christmas together with my husband, Ray. We were married in August 1979 and, at that time, Babycham was the modern day equivalent of Prosecco. It was used for celebrations and as a mixer. My husband and me never drank this bottle that Christmas so we put it away with the decorations and decided to keep it as a souvenir of our first Christmas together. My husband passed away five years ago and it is now on a shelf reminding me of all the good times we shared."

JANET KELLY

## Papal Visit Loo Seat

"This is a memento of Pope John Paul II's visit to the Phoenix Park in September, 1979. The week before the big day, we went with my father to see how the preparations were going. The new Papal Cross was impressive but as teenagers we were far more intrigued with the construction of rows and rows of long drop toilets by teams of carpenters. No portaloos back then! Oval shapes were cut at regular intervals from plywood benches large enough for a bottom, but not so large as to lose a small child. Plywood walls were erected to form cubicles and doors were added later. We took home this oval cut out and it has been used ever since as a breadboard or pot stand, not lavished with care but well used and certainly a family treasure. On the day of the papal mass in 1979, we revisited the toilets. The queues were massive, but we were very relieved with the facilities."

HELEN BACON

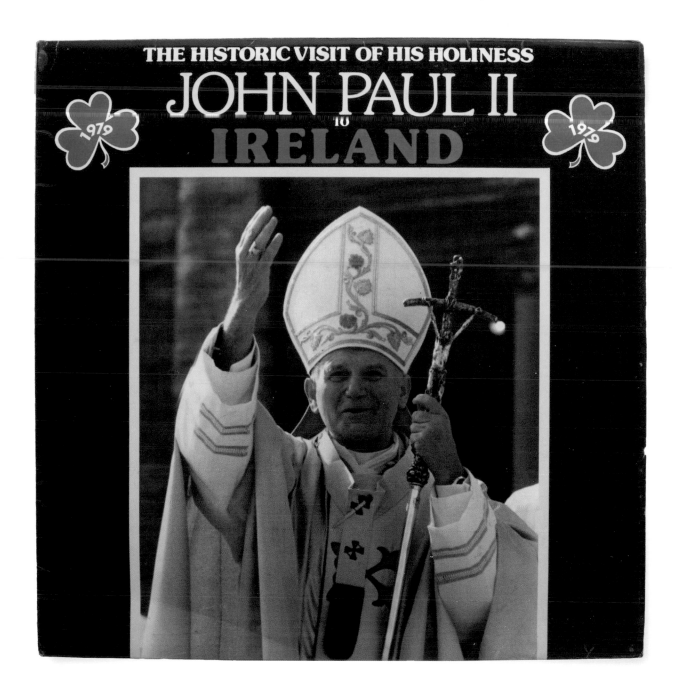

## Pope's Visit on Vinyl

"This is a recording of Pope John Paul ll's visit to Ireland in word and song. It records his speeches, his arrival in Dublin Airport, the Phoenix Park, Drogheda, Knock, and Galway. My sister, Marie Keogh, had this in her house and I inherited them from her after she died. I was at the Phoenix Park myself. When you applied to go see the pope, you were given a ticket and certain corrals. I was in the same corral as the rest of my family. If you had a deck chair, you brought it with you but mine was rusty and it collapsed, so I had to stand all day! I remember the plane flying over and the crowd waving at it. The pope then arrived by helicopter from Dublin Airport. I couldn't get very close to the pope, but I could see the pope-mobile. It was a great occasion with some beautiful hymns. I hold onto this object as a memory of the great occasion with my family. It was a great moment in my life and if I need to relive it again, I play this record."

VINCENT KEOGH

## "U2 at McGonagles" Poster

"In the late 70s while I was in school, I worked in a small sweet shop in Grafton Court where Murray's Record Shop and Captain America's was. The shop was at the front. U2 and other bands such as DC Nein, the Atrix, and the Virgin Prunes vied for space to hang their posters. Bono was always scrounging for small rolls of Sellotape from me. One day, he came in and I said, "No more, this is the last time," while winding Sellotape around a small plastic coin bag. He said, "I'll pay you back when I'm rich and famous." We both laughed! I can't remember why I held on to this poster but I'm glad I did."

JACKIE CRONIN

## Self-Aid Ticket and Programme

"This is a Self-Aid Ticket and Programme I got when I went to the Self-Aid gig in the RDS on 17th of May 1986. Unemployment was huge in the mid-80s and this concert was held to highlight the issue and raise money for job creation in Ireland. The concert included all of the big Irish acts at the time including Brush Shields, the Pogues, and the Boomtown Rats. The highlight for me was U2, who were already a huge international band at that stage. The event showed that during this grim time, young people could work together to create something positive."

CHRIS FARRELL

## Wood Quay Protest March Poster

"Wood Quay in Dublin had one of the best preserved Viking sites in Ireland and before the Dublin Civic Offices were built on top of them, there were many very active protest marches in favour of keeping the sites open. I was a student in Trinity at the time and had been involved in various protests on a range of international issues. Because this was a local issue and both my parents were proud Dubliners, it was something that was very close to my heart. Concrete won in the end! Politics won! The people lost."

KEVIN ECOCK

### Johnny Logan's "What's Another Year!" Single

"This is an original single for 'What's Another Year!' the song that launched Johnny Logan into Eurovision folklore when he won the competition in 1980. This was my brother's record and it was passed on to me. Johnny Logan was the first Irish winner that I witnessed and it was a huge family event, one of the few things we all watched together. Back then, winning was a huge honour and it was a difficult thing to do. For Ireland to be so good at it was a big deal and perhaps it's only in hindsight now that you realise how good we actually were. I watch the Eurovision now with my own family and it's still a big event in my house."

DÓNALL DUNNE

## A2 Silkscreen Poster for Flikkers Ball at the Hirschfeld Centre

"Flikkers was the disco at the Hirschfeld Centre, Dublin, which was opened on Fownes St. in 1979 by the National Gay Federation. The community centre was the first full-time lesbian and gay venue in Ireland. It housed a meeting space, a youth group, a café, a small cinema and film club and it ran discos at the weekend where gay men, lesbian women, and transgender people socialised. Somewhere like the Hirschfeld centre provided a massive service and it was a bulwark against wider social exclusion. The centre, which was one of the earliest of its kind in the world, burned down in 1987 in un-proven circumstances. This poster, the first publicly commissioned work of designer Niall Sweeney, was rescued from the building. Its edges are burnt and scorched and you can still smell the smoke."

TONIE WALSH

# Carrickmacross Lace Veil

"My father was born in Carrickmacross, Co. Monaghan and he frequently brought us to his home county to visit relations. Over the years, I looked with interest at one of my cousins making lace and admired the finished pieces. The year before my daughter Amy made her First Holy Communion in 1983, I made a few trips to Carrickmacross and my cousin patiently taught me how to make lace. When I had mastered the basics, I started making a veil. It was hard work that required patience, concentration, good eyesight, and perseverance, and this is the result. I think it's really important to recognise that this cottage industry had a significant impact for a small part of Ireland and how the production of these beautiful items provided a well-needed additional source of income for many families during hard economic times."

MARGARET RIORDAN

## Local Election Poster

"'A local character made good.' This is an election poster for Bernie Murphy, the former Cork City Councillor and self-styled 'People's Champion'. He was one of the great characters in Irish life and this poster captures how a bit of mischief became reality. Bernie was originally a walking advertisement and he could be found parading the South Mall in Cork City with a sandwich board. Everybody in Cork knew him as he was such a permanent fixture. In 1985, it was rumoured that a few people associated with the legal profession decided to give Bernie a makeover (as seen in the poster) and put him on the ballot in the local elections. At one stage during the election campaign, Bernie was on the back of a 40-foot trailer with a coterie of well-dolled out dancing girls travelling around Cork City. A huge amount of betting was placed on Bernie; at one stage he was 50/1 to be elected, and when he came in second on the ballot, a local bookmaker lost a lot of money. After the election, Cork had been twinned with San Francisco and as a councillor Bernie went to San Francisco and somehow came back with an honorary doctorship and a new set of false teeth. He became known locally as Dr. Teeth from then. When he was originally elected, many people were concerned that he'd make a mockery of the City Council but he didn't. Bernie did his full stint as a councillor and was not a source of embarrassment. He ultimately failed to be re-elected as a councillor in 1985 (he had previously tried to be elected to the Dáil as well but was unsuccessful). He eventually returned to walking the South Mall with his sandwich board and eventually passed away in 2007. He definitely was the only real Cork candidate!"

AONGHUS O'BROIN

## Sinn Féin
## Christmas Cards

"These are Christmas cards sent to me by my brother, Emmet, in Dublin when I was living in Sydney, probably in 1984. When I received them, I thought, "Oh my god," because they were highly unusual, to say the least. On the back of one of them, he wrote, "Hang this on the wall of your front hall so that everybody can see it and ask about it." Emmet was ill throughout his life and read a lot while in hospital, including about Sinn Féin. He became a member of Sinn Féin and was an activist in Ballyfermot. He has since died and these Christmas Cards are a memory of him in many ways."

ANGELA BLOUNT

## Euro '88 Jersey and Memorabilia

"I was 14 at the time of Euro '88 and my Father happened to be working in Germany that summer. Tickets for the games, especially the England match, were like gold dust, but we managed to get one for myself, my father, and my brother, Brendan. Going to Stuttgart that summer was a huge deal for me at that young age and it was a huge occasion for the nation as whole because Euro 88 was the first time Ireland qualified for a major football championship. During the England match, Ray Houghton scored after six minutes and the Irish fans went crazy. I'll never forget it. Thankfully, Ireland managed to hold off the English attack for the rest of the game. That summer was the start of the glory days of Irish soccer with Jack Charlton and the Irish fans becoming the toast of Germany. I think that was the beginning of a worldwide love for visiting Irish soccer fans that has carried right through until today. I still tell my own kids about going to this match and I remember every single detail of that famous time."

MICHEÁL NEWELL

## Euro '88 Tickets

"Christy Moore has a song called, "Joxer goes to Stuttgart" and we had a very similar story to Joxer. Myself and a gang of friends travelled to see the Irish soccer team play in Euro '88, and it was a lifelong dream to see the Boys in Green at the finals of a major championship. Our very first game, we were up against our old rivals England and we beat them. There were about 12,000 Irish fans there and it was all pretty wild. In many ways, it was a loss of our football virginity, a completely different experience for both us and the Irish team. I was reasonably untraveled at the time so it was a very new experience. The Ireland vs. English match ticket stub is signed by Paul McGrath and Mick McCarthy. One of these tickets is sadly an unused semi-final ticket."

PATRICK PETERS

# An Post's "Cassette Post"

"Before the mobile phone, An Post brought out cassette tapes so that you could send voice messages to family and friends abroad. I bought three of them at the time and sent one to a brother of mine in Manchester. The other two I kept and remain unused. Each cassette had seven and a half minutes of recording on each side. As a means of communication, Cassette Post had a short life. Maybe in 40 or 50 years, they might be saying the same thing about mobile phones."

VINCENT GRAY

## Motorola Mobile Phone

"This is a Motorola mobile telephone bought in Dublin in the 1980s. It was very expensive to buy at the time. I worked in the haulage industry and this device made communication much easier for us. Previously, we used landlines and we would have to stop at phone boxes so as to ring home to see if there were any new loads to be picked up. As a result, we could be using a phone box every hour or so. When I travelled the continent, it was the same thing. Sometimes we had to sit waiting at a phone box for hours, until someone had a load for us. That was the only communication we used back then and there would always be drivers going back and forth to phone boxes all the time. Before the mobile phone, I remember when I drove home from Cork, my wife used to ring the Garda Station in Mitchelstown and they would stop me to tell me to ring home about a new load to be picked up. Sometimes I had to turn around and go back to Cork. If it wasn't the guards, someone might know someone else on the way who my wife could ring and they would do their best to make contact with me. When mobile phone technology arrived, it was fantastic. This phone may have felt like carrying a concrete brick and the reception wasn't great either, but it was a hell of a lot better than hanging around phone boxes. I haven't used a phone box in over 30 years."

PATRICK AYLWARD

## Bottle of Blue Nun, Unopened, circa 1986

"The German wines Blue Nun and Black Tower were pretty much the most quintessentially "Irish wine" of the 1980s and 1990s. Le Piat d'Or French wine was another early exponent. I've no idea how this bottle remained unopened in our house for such a long time. My Aunt Kathleen Malone discovered it at the back of a cupboard. She bought it in Superquinn, Naas, and I often laugh at the fact that the bottle has lasted longer than the supermarket itself."

TOM LAWLER

## Bootleg Cassettes

"These cassettes are DIY live recordings of concerts from circa 1980s. They include great Irish and International bands playing in Ireland such as Bjork, the Divine Comedy, and the Waterboys. Pre-internet, these cassettes were the best way of hearing songs from bands that were not yet released. They were often a piece of memorabilia from a concert you were at or a way to hear songs from an un-signed, up-and- coming Irish band. Quality was varied because this was usually recorded by people in the crowd. They were normally sold by street traders on O'Connell Bridge or in independent record stores. The design of the cassette involved luminous coloured paper with black-and-white photocopying on-top. These days, younger generations would capture these recordings immediately using smart phones but these objects are a relic of a different generation."

PATRICK GRIFFIN

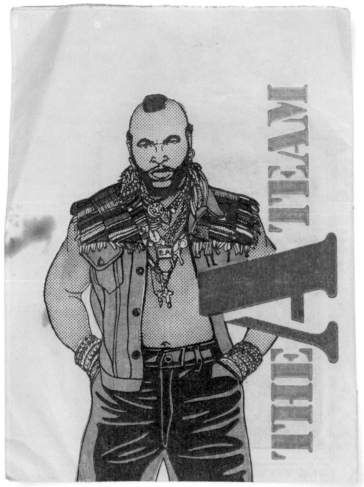

## A-Team
## Collectible Cards

"When I was a child I collected comics, toy soldiers and other items. Myself and my friends would always have swapped objects with each other. Years later when I was in my early thirties and had young children of my own I came across these A-Team cards in a shop and I got an urge to buy a number of packets. The cards came inside the envelope (Pictured with Mr T on it) and they also included chewing gums. I used to watch the *A-Team* back in those days and always liked that it was entertaining and full of action but nobody ever actually got killed. It was great viewing for kids and adults alike. When I heard about the National Treasures project I dug out these cards as for me they are indicative of the arrival of eighties American pop culture into Ireland. Programmes like the *A-Team*, *Airwolf* and *Knightrider* were a staple on many Irish television sets on Saturdays in the eighties and these cards bring back fond memories for many people."

PATRICK AMBROSE

## Mr. Crow Moneybox

"Before Permanent TSB came to Ballincollig, there was a bank called the Cork Savings Bank. When kids like myself opened their account there in the 1980s, they were given a Mr Crow money box so that they could save at home. I remember my grandfather taking me on the ten-mile trip into Ballincollig to open my new account. I was seven or eight and this was the first time I had any responsibility in my life. I put money in the box every week and then we went to the bank with my money and lodgement book once or twice a year and put it into my account. I was a really good saver. Last year, we had a leak in the hot press in our house and Mr Crow resurfaced when it was getting fixed. He'd been hiding in there for nearly thirty years. It's a nice little piece of history that is unique to the Cork area and will evoke happy childhood memories for many people from that era."

SÍLE HUNT

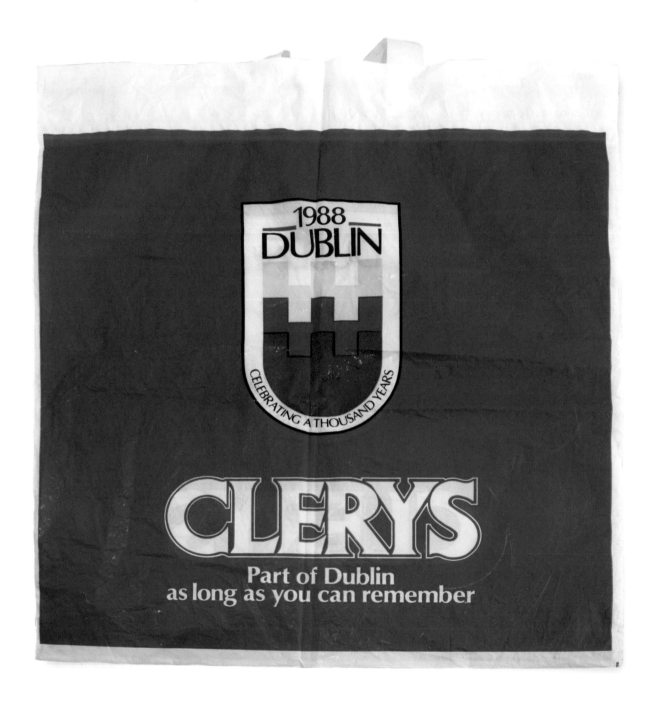

## Clerys 1988 Plastic Bag

"This plastic Clerys bag reads "Part of Dublin as long as you can remember" and features a logo of the Dublin 1988 Millennium Commemoration, a huge event at the time. The bag belonged to my mother and was found in her house in a box. It is still in very neat condition. Clery's is closed now and no longer part of Dublin, but I'm sure that many people all across Ireland have held on to their plastic bags."

LINDA CASEY

## Dublin 1988 Millennium Fire Screen

"I was a teacher in Coláiste Eoin, Finglas and there was a transition year project to encourage pupils to start their own business. They had a variety of items and I bought this one.

I think it cost 40 pounds. I needed a fire screen, which is why I bought it. 1988 was such a big year for Dublin and all sorts of memorabilia was created. We don't have too many ornaments in the house, but this fire screen has been a permanent fixture."

ANGELA CONWAY

## Poster from Galway's First Gay Pride Parade

"In 1988, when I was in my early twenties, there were practically no supports for the gay/lesbian community in the west of Ireland, so along with four other women, I helped found the gay/lesbian helpline in Galway city. It was an extremely difficult task to get this service up and running and many challenges were overcome to get a venue and make our vision a reality. After launch, the helpline was immediately deemed a success, providing support to people all along the west coast of Ireland. A few years later in 1990, I witnessed a number of my older lesbian friends travelling to London for the Pride celebrations. I told myself that I didn't want to march in a Pride Parade anywhere, until I was able to do so in my own city of Galway. This drove me to begin organising the first Pride Parade in Galway and with the help of a group of friends, including Jane Talbot (who designed this poster), we made a banner and organised a time and place. It was very difficult to get people involved as many of my friends were not openly gay and were not comfortable with attending such a public event. The parade went ahead and, along with fourteen other people, most of whom were heterosexual, we took part in the west of Ireland's first ever Pride Parade. This event has taken place in Galway every year since and now it is just one part of a week-long Pride festival."

NUALA WARD

## "An Appalling Vista"

"I bought this limited edition print by artist, Robert Ballagh, to support a fundraising campaign aimed at launching a legal challenge to overturn the wrongful conviction of the Birmingham Six. In the House of Lords in 1980, Lord Denning said that no sane person would believe that the British police force and judiciary would conspire to keep innocent people in jail; he said it would be, "An appalling vista." This is therefore the title given to this print. I paid 80 or 90 pounds in 1989 and I was very passionate about this issue. It was obvious that these men were setup and I felt that enough is enough. They were freed in 1991."

MICHAEL HALLEY

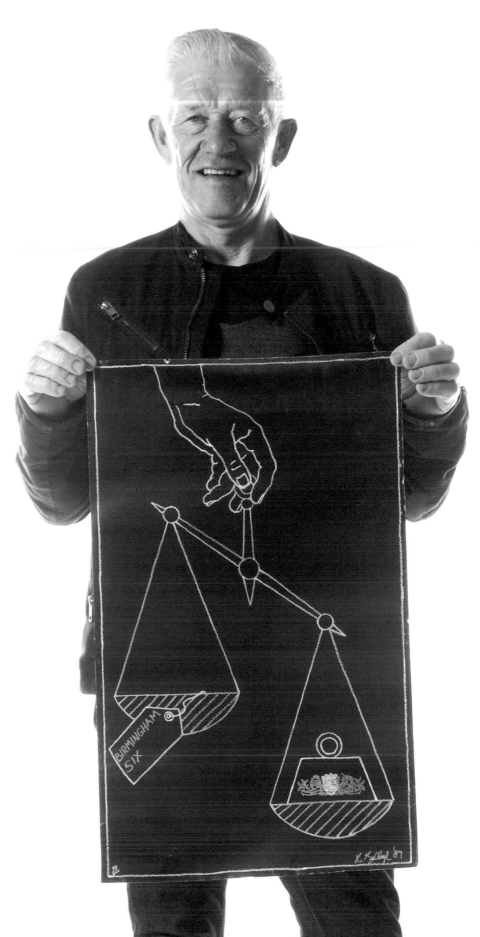

## Sean Kelly's Hat

"This signed hat by Irish cyclist Sean Kelly has some story to tell. At the time, the country was cycling mad! Sean Kelly, Stephen Roche, and Martin Earley were at the top of their game on the world stage. The Nissan International Cycling Classic was a five-day event that started and finished in Dublin .The first stage in 1990 was from Dublin to Waterford and took place on the 10th of October. It was the time of German reunification and all the German cyclists were given a presentation. I had just started my first year in De La Salle College and we were all on a half day so that we could go and see the stage finish into Waterford City on the Mall. I was with some schoolmates and we were nicely positioned just after the finish line. One of the lads dared me to get Waterford hero Sean Kelly's hat and I set about this. He was riding for PDM Ultima at the time and the gear was very much in vogue. Less than two minutes after Kelly crossed the line in fifth place, I grabbed his hat and he still chased me even after being in the saddle for hours. He caught up with me and was very annoyed. One of my friends' fathers who was with us persuaded Kelly to let me have the hat, which he kindly did. Later that evening, we headed up to the Ard Rí Hotel where all the teams were staying overnight. We saw Kelly come in and I asked him if he would sign the hat, and he did so with a rueful smile. Now that's a classic and that is a national treasure of a story to tell."

MICHAEL O'CONNOR

## Galway Football Jersey 1991

"This is my jersey from when I played in the Vocational Schools All-Ireland Final in 1991. Up until that day, logos on jerseys were forbidden by the GAA but they had just brought in regulations to allow for sponsorship. These guidelines came into effect on the day of our match, the 5th of May, 1991. Our jersey on the day was sponsored by 'Galway Oil'. We played before the National League Final between Dublin and Kildare (who also had sponsors), therefore it is the first regulated sponsored jersey in GAA history. It represents a turning point in the sport when sponsors decided to get involved. Ever since, sponsorship has been part and parcel of the GAA. It has changed the game, allowing for better facilities and better support for players. If there is one downside, perhaps it has made the game more uneven with bigger, more successful counties attracting larger corporate sponsors."

RAYMOND O'DOWD

## "Last Supper"

"Women were first allowed to vote in Great Britain and Ireland in 1918. Mary Robinson was elected the first woman President of Ireland in 1990. The Church of Ireland voted to allow women priests in 1990. This painting of the "Last Supper" with men, women and children present was commissioned by the Irish group BASIC (Brothers And Sisters In Christ) who support women priests in the Roman Catholic Church. In 1999, a framed copy of this "Last Supper" was presented by BASIC to President Mary McAleese at Áras an Uachtaráin. In 2001, the first "Women's Ordination Worldwide" conference was held in Dublin. To mark this international conference, this version of the "Last Supper" was placed on seven billboards around Ireland. I was a member of BASIC and I commissioned this from a Polish artist, Bohdan Piaseeki. Some people say that it is an alternative "Last Supper" but looking at historical documents, it is actually more accurate than Leonard Di Vinci's "Last Supper". In our "Last Supper", people are eating with their right hands, they are wearing Jewish clothes, and both women and children are present."

COLM HOLMES

## Belfast Community Circus School's Bed of Nails

"My husband, Mike Moloney, was one of the founders of the Belfast Community Circus School in 1985. Mike was originally from Toowoomba, Australia and had trained as a drama teacher. He came to Ireland in 1981, and within a couple of years, started doing workshops teaching unicycling, juggling, stilt walking, rolla bolla, and acrobalance. Mike met Donal McKendry, who was also a performer, and they began, along with myself, running a regular Saturday workshop in the Ormeau Recreation Centre in 1985. This was the beginning of the Belfast Community Circus School, which went on to grow and grow. They now have a purpose built school with classes running daily. During the 1980s, the circus was not seen as something you did or learned, but something that you visited and went to watch. There was nowhere in Ireland to train as a circus performer, and it was Mike's vision that pioneered this and changed people's perspectives of the circus as a possible career."

NORA GREER

## Zig and Zag
## Christmas No.1 Tape

"Myself and my sisters received this as a Christmas present from our parents. I was a huge fan of Zig and Zag, everyone was a big fan. You had to be because they were hilarious! Zig and Zag were the big kids' TV stars of the 80s and 90s and we watched them every day after school. This song was a Christmas rap and they had a very funny video to go with it. I no longer have a tape player but I still have this tape. I could never throw it out; it's a memory of my childhood and I still share ownership with my sisters!"

AILISE O'LOUGHLIN

## Zig and Zag Annuals

"Like any child in the 1990s, Zig and Zag were a huge part of growing up and I regularly watched them with my brother Tiarnán. We really loved how unfiltered and entertaining they were and how it was unashamedly Irish. For me, these were the glory days of kids' television when programmes like Zig and Zag were just as good, if not better, than other content coming from the UK or America. We were absolutely devastated when Zig and Zag moved to Channel 4 and we could no longer watch them. Every Christmas, my brother and me got the yearly annuals and these two pictured are the only ones that I have left. Zig and Zag might be long gone now, but we recently watched some old videos of them on YouTube and I think they are still as funny as ever."

CAOIMHE MCDONOUGH

# Thank You

All those who participated, John Creedon, Tony Candon, Sarah Ryder, Aifric Ní Chianáin, Tracey Diamond, Donal Fallon, Roisín Higgins, Richard McElligott, Linda King, Ruth Griffin and Michael Fortune, Frances Toner, Ann Daly, Isobel Nolan, Dave Bolger, Derek Merren, Dave Fleming, Fionnuala Mac Aodha, Susan Scannell, Bríd Browne, Jill Kane, Adrian Lynch, Maurice Linnane, Anne-Marie Kelly, Tara Doyle, Dublin City Libraries, Brendan McGowan, Galway City Museum, Hannah Crowdy, National Museums Northern Ireland, Laura McCorry, Philip Cooper, Nuala Dormer, Deirdre Laird, Natalie Clarke, Deirdre Learmont, Dean-Ross Murray, Aline Biz, Paul Kelly, Michael Fleming, Alan Farquharson, Paul Giles, Colm Giles, Tony Donoghue, Dave Greaney, Barry O'Reilly, Business to Arts, Claire Fitzgerald, Donal Hall, Neil Devlin, Lisa Kearns, Rebecca Bermingham, Margaret Gibbons, Colm Quinn, Yvonne Seery, Active Retirement Ireland, Irish Countrywomen's Association, Carole Holohan, John O'Sullivan, Jim Gillespie, Ross O'Callaghan, Michael Fleming, Paul Kerney, Dan Dalton, Gerry MacArthur, Martin Birney, Brian Moore, Joe Edwards, Ciaran Tanham, Emmet Harte, Deirdre O'Toole, Conor Lally, Garr Cleary, Cathal O'Friel, Joseph Mylotte, Michael Casey, Pearl Phelan, Eoin O'Conaill, Eoin Cooke, Stephen McDowell, Daniel Gaughran, Andrew Wilson, Trevor Cunningham, Amy McDowell, Ronan McMeel, Fionnuala Mac Aodha, Susan Scannell, Deirdre Learmont, Linda Logan, Janine Curran, Eleanor Nolan, Sylvia Lynch, Shireen Langan, Ruth McCarthy, Warren Hall, Stephanie Brien, Candice Devine, Tra My Nguyen, Niamh Ní Riain, Maeve Donovan, Alice Mauger, Donagh Mac Uidhir, Victoria Franco Martin, Kayne Coy, Aisling Coffey, Béibhinn Ní Neachtain, Billy Keenan, Leah Kane, Leanne Hanafin, Lucien Waugh-Daly, Neil Reilly, Rachael Martin, Robert Cooper, Sarah Mangan, Sibéal Ní Mhaoileoin, Harvey Hines, Gabrielle Deeny, Ciara McLarnon, Aoibhin Synnott, Colm Moloney, Luka Phelan, Shamim Malekmian, Catapult Events, Michael Higgins, Kevin Corry, Keith Alexander, Brian Gormley, Jessica Gorman, Vicky Moran, Paul Kelly, Brian McMahon, Garry O'Neill, Colm Martin, Anne O'Dowd, Sally Roden, Derek O'Connor, Gareth Naughton, Bernie Cullinan, Gaye Maguire, Anne-Marie Kelly, Mairead Heffernan, Philip Cooper, Maeve Rogan, Paul Allison, Ross Cullen, Tony McCarthy, Tonie Walsh, Mary Clancy, Andrew Hetherington, Tanya Kiang, Sandra Austin, Susan Pike, Joe Guilfoyle, Peter Kavanagh, Cliona O'Carroll, Brand New Retro, Irish Election Literature, Ye Olde Hurdy Gurdy Museum of Vintage Radio, Rainbow Ballroom of Romance, Festival of History, Marino Institute of Education, National Print Museum, Irish Linen Centre, Frank McCourt Museum, The Butter Museum, Northern Ireland Family, Historical Society, The Computers and Communications Museum, North Mayo Heritage Centre, Cobh Museum, Kate's Cottage, Irish Men's Sheds Association.